Intarsia
Workbook

by Judy Gale Roberts
and Jerry Booher

Fox
Chapel Publishing

1970 Broad Street • East Petersburg, PA 17520
www.FoxChapelPublishing.com

Intarsia Workbook is an original work, first published in 2003 by Fox Chapel Publishing Company, Inc. The patterns contained herein are copyrighted by the author. Artists may make up to three photocopies of each individual pattern for personal use. The patterns themselves, however, are not to be duplicated for resale or distribution under any circumstances. This is a violation of copyright law.

Publisher	Alan Giagnocavo
Cover Design	Jon Deck
Desktop Specialist	Linda Eberly, Eberly Designs

ISBN 1–56523–226–7

To learn more about the other great books
from Fox Chapel Publishing, or to find a
retailer near you, call toll-free 1-800-457-9112
or visit us at **www.FoxChapelPublishing.com.**

Printed in China
10 9 8 7 6 5 4 3 2

Table of Contents

Introduction 1

Project One
   Bow 4

Project Two
   Bow and Bells 20

Project Three
   Whale 30

Project Four
   Sea Gull in Flight 42

Project Five
   Sea Gull Landing 54

Project Six
   Chicken Pair 62

Project Seven
   Apple with Worm 72

Project Eight
   Hot Air Balloon 82

Introduction

This lesson book combines Jerry Booher's scroll sawing/precision skills and my, Judy Gale Roberts, wood selection and shaping skills. Over the past 20 years we have perfected the techniques we use and are able to verbally express those skills so others may learn from our experiences. Teaching Intarsia classes for the last four years has proven beneficial to our teaching skills.

Working so closely with each student, I have a much clearer understanding of what being a beginner to intarsia feels like. Our first class was a real eye opener for myself, as well as for Jerry. I have been working with wood in this manner for so many years I had forgotten most of the struggles I went through to get here. With the advent of a "Workbook" we are able to put these types of lessons together to help you get a solid basic foundation to build on. We hope you enjoy the lessons in this book and believe they will give you a well-rounded understanding of Intarsia that will help you with all your future projects.

I use mainly Western red cedar, although any type of wood can be used. Western red cedar can be found in a variety of colors, from an almost white to a black/brown. The white is the sap wood of the tree, and I believe the darker shades are in the center of the tree. The cedar is generally shipped wet, so you will need to dry your wood before using it. These are huge trees that grow in the northwestern United States and in Canada. It is commonly used for fence pickets, siding and decks mostly in the south, eastern and northeastern regions of the U.S. The color and grain patterns are more important than the type of wood used. It takes many trips to the lumberyard before I have the variety of tones needed to make a larger Intarsia project. You will want to get an assortment of colors, as well as some boards with straighter grain patterns and some with more unique/curly grains. Using a combination of curly and straight grains can give the project balance. The straight grains balance your project and help the more exotic grain stand out. If you were making a bird, perhaps you would use the most unusual grain on the wing and a more subtle grain on the rest of the bird. Most of the unusual grains are found around knots. Boards that are full of knots have the most character. These boards also end up at the bottom of the pile, because most people do not want the boards that are full of knots. When you are "breaking in" a lumberyard, it is a good idea to bring pictures of what you plan to do with

the wood. Let them know you are not looking for the "best" boards. We also keep them happy by leaving the stack neater than it was when we arrived. There have only been a few lumberyards that have not allowed us to look through the wood.

I use aspen for a white wood; it stays a nice warm white color even after the finish has been applied. If you are impatient and want to get started before you have a variety of wood shades, a little stain goes a long way. Especially when you are first getting started, it's a good way to get the practice in before you start spending a small fortune on wood.

If you choose to use hardwoods or exotic woods, keep in mind it's the shades or tones to look for rather than the color. Dark walnut can be used for areas marked "D" (Dark shade); mahogany, cherry and pecan can be used for "MD" (Medium Dark shade); maple and birch can be used for "M" (Medium shade); white oak, some birch and some basswood can be used for "LT" (Light shade); poplar, holly, aspen and white pine can be used for "W" (white shade).

I cannot even begin to suggest any exotic woods, there are far too many varieties that I am not aware of. I would suggest, however, finding out as much as possible about each species of wood to see if they may be carcinogenic. Always wear a dust mask regardless of what type of wood you are working.

Part of the excitement with Intarsia is exploring all the beauty in wood, analyzing grain configurations along with color. Once you get tuned into the grain patterns and colors, you will never look at wood the same. We tried putting up a small cedar fence, and I kept claiming all the boards. We had to buy more pickets to finish the fence. Wood that varies in color from one edge to the other are a terrific find for Intarsia. I have had the opportunity to work with some spalted wood and some burls that work especially great for beards and hair. The possibilities are endless; sometimes the wood inspires a project, and other times the shaping of the wood surprises me with a perfect grain for that particular part.

The lessons in this book will help you to get acquainted with Intarsia. The first lesson is a bow cut out of the same material. It is easier to cut out than the other projects and does not require a large selection of wood. You can get started right away. From there, the projects gradually get a little more complex, adding more colors, parts and dimension. If you are new to Intarsia, I suggest you start with Lesson One and work your way through to Lesson Eight. Each project requires more experience and practice using different techniques that I use everyday. These projects are designed with a scroll saw in mind, however they could be modified for use on a bandsaw. On each pattern you will notice a legend showing grain direction, tones of wood colors, and areas marked for raising with ¼" shims.

The following are some helpful ideas to keep in mind for these projects and for any Intarsia projects you make in the future.

- I use mainly Western red cedar, though any type of wood can be used. The color and grain patterns are more important than the type of wood used. When going to a lumberyard to look for Western red cedar, be sure to ask for it by its entire name. Many times it is confused with the Eastern cedar or aromatic red cedar that is used in closets and other similar applications. Look at the fence pickets; it seems there is a larger variety of shades that end up there.
- I use aspen for a white wood, because it stays a nice warm white color even after the finish has been applied.
- Make all copies of the pattern at the same time, because not all copiers are created the same. Copies from one machine may stretch the pattern one way or another. Even using the same copier from day to day can show distortions.
- Always check both sides of the board when you layout your pieces. Sometimes a knot may angle into the part. Also, if using the natural highlight in a certain board, check both sides of the wood,— even the edge grain if possible—to see how deep the lighter color goes.
- My theory for laying the pattern parts onto the wood is as follows. I put what would be the main pattern parts on the wood first giving them top priority. Then I place the other parts around it. Take a pattern of a horse's head as an example. I would put the major parts of the horse head in the best grain placement possible, then fill in with the secondary parts of the same color: like ears. Using the paper pattern cut up in sections makes this process much easier. You can really move the pattern pieces around to get the best grain for each part.

- Make sure your lumber is dry. A moisture meter is a good investment.
- When you are sanding your project, keep it as close to the sander as possible. Also keep all the parts assembled and check often before removing more material. I have a cart on wheels that I put right next to the sander. If I have any doubt as to where to sand a part, I can look at the project and refresh my memory. (As I age this seems to happen more and more.) I will mark on the surface (with a pencil) areas that need to be sanded. Give yourself all the indicators you can think of. As we all know once it's gone you cannot put it back.

A Word About Scroll Saw Blades

The question most often asked is, "What scroll saw blades do I use?"

What blades a scroller should use is a very difficult question to answer. Many times what works here in our shop for our saws and our type of material may not work for someone else.

Let's start with pin-end blades. Usually pin-end blades are included on entry-level saws. The downside to them is that there are very few blades available from which to choose. The size of pin-end blades is also another factor; they have to be large in order for the pin to fit in the blade. This pin fastens the blade to the saw. The larger blade will limit the turning ability of the blade and the size of inside cuts because of the large hole that must be drilled to accommodate the pin.

Plain-end blades are the most popular blades, and there are many different ones available, from very tiny (like the hairs on your head) to very large. There are several manufactures of these blades, and almost all of them have their own tooth styles and configurations. For that reason, it is difficult to suggest a blade that will work for you on all materials. In many cases, choosing your blades may take much experimentation to decide which one works best for you. I can tell you one thing: For me there is not one blade that will last all day or just one blade that I use for all materials and thicknesses. Through experience I have chosen blades that work best for me on the different materials and thicknesses that I use.

Normally I use a universal #5 for most of my sawing

of ¾" or less. For slicing-up parts, I will use a #2 or smaller blade, depending on the material I am cutting. For thicker material I will use a #7 blade. As a general rule of thumb, the thicker the wood, the higher the blade number.

Not only are there different sizes of blades, there are also different tooth configurations that you can choose. There are regular tooth blades; skip tooth blades, where every other tooth is eliminated giving more chip clearance; reverse skip tooth blades, where there are five to seven teeth at the bottom of the blade that reverse in direction; and even a round blade that will cut in all different directions. Personally I use mostly reverse skip tooth blades. The reverse teeth are on bottom when the blade is mounted in the saw, and the blade cuts on the upstroke as well as on the downstroke. Reverse tooth blades may have a tendency to lift the part up on the upstroke. Reverse tooth blades also usually give a cleaner finish on the bottom side of the part.

As you can see, choosing a blade can be a very difficult and time-consuming task. The best advice I can give is to get a big fistful of blades and a stack of lumber and start cutting. Experience is the best thing you can use.

Saw Speed

Another difficult thing to explain is how fast to run your saw. Again, what is comfortable for me may not be comfortable for you. Most saws today are variable speed with a maximum of 1,600 to 1,800 strokes per minute. As a rule, I run between 70 and 80 percent of the full speed range. That's not to say that I never run full speed, that's just where I feel comfortable and have my best accuracy. Experiment to find the best speed for the material and blade you are using as well as for your comfort when sawing.

We hope you enjoy the lessons in this book and believe they will give you a solid foundation for all your future Intarsia projects.

—Judy Gale Roberts and Jerry Booher

Lesson One

Bow

In this lesson you will learn the fundamentals of shaping your projects. You will sand lower parts to give the bow dimension. Also, you will learn how to apply a great professional finish.

TOOLS:

- Scroll saw or bandsaw
- #5 reverse skip tooth blades
- Sander for contouring, (Softer is better. A pneumatic (air-inflated) sander is best, however a belt sander or disc sander will work also.)
- Carving knife or woodburner (optional)

MATERIALS:

- A medium shade of wood, at least 6½" W x 7½" L x ¼" D
- Repositionable spray adhesive or glue stick
- At least two copies of the Bow pattern
- ¼" Luan plywood for the backing
- Woodworkers glue

Pattern Preparation/Layout

Before I start working on any project, I study the pattern. This is a good habit to learn. It will help you to be able to anticipate any problems that may arise ahead of time thus making your work more enjoyable. Glance over the Bow pattern on page 6. This lesson is fairly easy; however, the basics for simple to complex projects are the same. On smaller patterns I glue copies of the pattern to the wood, rather than using carbon paper to transfer each section to the wood. This eliminates any human error, as far as the layout goes. The bow pattern has only one color of wood, and all the grain directions are the same. This tells me that I will need just one copy of the pattern to make the Bow. I like to make a couple of extra copies: one for my master and an extra one just in case. If you do not have wood wide enough to put the pattern on in one piece (a 7" width for this project), you will need one more copy of the pattern, making a total of four copies.

Next I check what wood is involved. On the bow there is only one color, M, a medium shade of wood. Also studying the pattern I note there isn't a whole

Bow

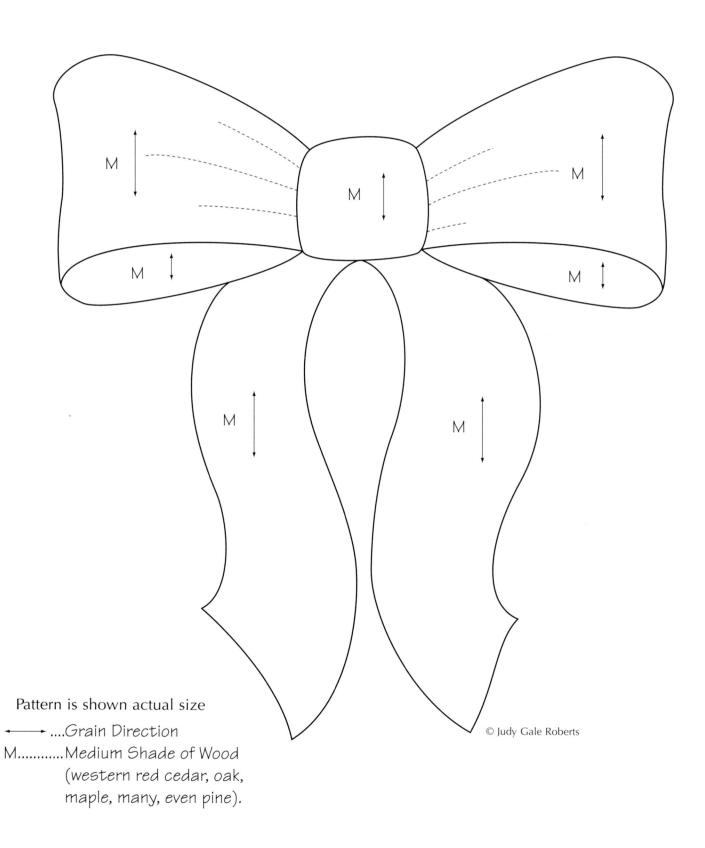

Pattern is shown actual size

←————→ ....Grain Direction

M............Medium Shade of Wood
(western red cedar, oak,
maple, many, even pine).

© Judy Gale Roberts

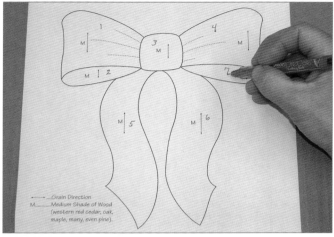

1.1

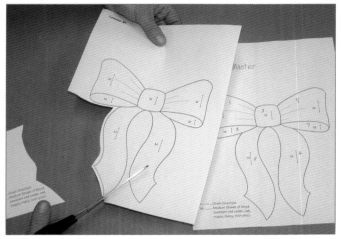

1.2

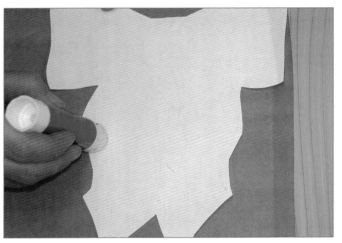

1.3

lot of detail. If I can find some really unusual grain patterns in a piece of wood, it will make the bow more interesting. Also, because the grain direction is the same, it will help if I use thicker wood, at least ¾" thick, so the bow will have much more depth. If I cut this out of ¼" thick wood and barely rounded it, the bow would look flat.

We use Western red cedar, which comes somewhat smooth on three sides: the face and both edges. We run the rough side through a planer, taking off just enough to make the board lie flat. Clean up both sides if needed; I am always trying to conserve the thickness of the wood. You can use whatever wood you have on hand for this project. Remember: This is one of many lessons; we are not striving for the perfect bow on the first lesson.

Label one of the pattern copies as your "master." I like to number the master, numbering each part con-

secutively for the bow **(see photo 1.1)**. Next take one of the copies and trim it, giving it about a ¼" border around the line work **(see photo 1.2)**. Transfer the numbers from the master onto the copy. Now we will glue the pattern to the wood **(see photo 1.3)**. I use a "re-stickable" glue stick. It is a water-based product that works great for me. A "repositionable" spray adhesive will do the job also. The trick with the glue stick is to let it dry about 20 to 30 seconds before putting it on the wood; then burnish it down for extra "stay power." It's better to use too much glue than not enough. There is nothing more frustrating than cutting a critical area and the paper starts flapping. (Just ask Jerry!) Also, I've noticed if any of the paper pattern is hanging over the wood, it will start to peel back. I trim any paper even with the edge of the board. Another thing I like to do is to mark up the pattern using arrows on all the outside edges **(see**

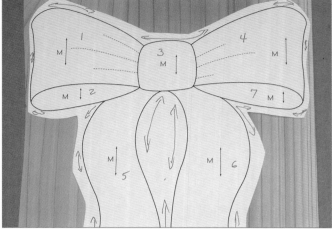

1.4

1.5

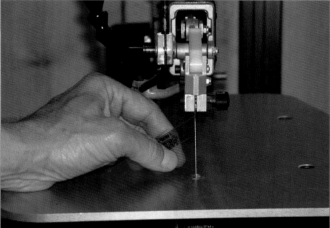

1.6

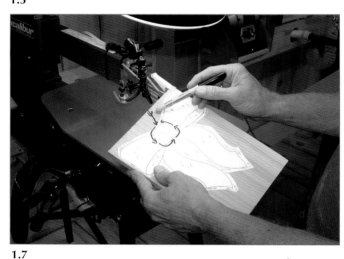

1.7

photo 1.4). This way, when you start sawing, you can saw the outside edges first. Nothing fits next to the outside parts, so you can relax a bit and get into the swing of sawing before you have to make any parts fit.

Scroll Sawing

There are two items I use on my scroll saw that I find very helpful. The first is a foot switch, which allows me to start and stop my saw while both hands are holding the part (see photo 1.5). The second is a magnifier/light, which provides ample light and magnifies the lines so I can see them much better.

Sawing a project such as this bow is pretty simple, because we will be using the same material. I use a scroll saw with a #5 blade, but you could use a bandsaw for this project. The #5 blade is pretty thin and the kerf, the space left behind as the blade cuts, is small compared with a bandsaw blade. Just remember:

When cutting a project apart and then putting it back together, the width of the kerf will make a difference in the fit.

Set up your scroll saw so the blade is square to the table. This can be done with a small square (see photo 1.6). This applies to both the scroll saw and the bandsaw.

Check the Material

Turn the piece of wood over and make sure that any burr or tear-out is removed from the back so the material will lie flat on the table. You can start sawing the project just about anywhere you would like, but I would start at the knot of the bow (see photo 1.7). By sawing this section first and then removing it, the rest of the bow can be cut without the fear of bumping into the knot with the blade (see photo 1.8). It would be best when sawing to put the

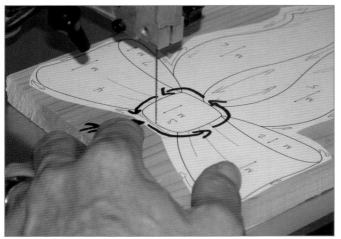
1.8

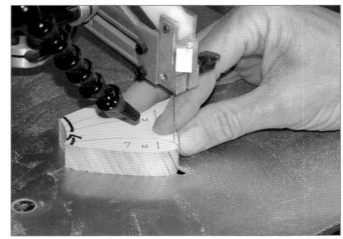
1.9

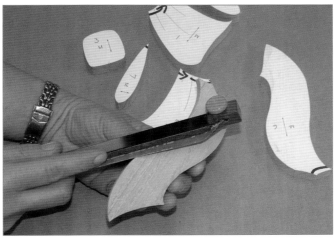
1.10

center of the blade on the center of the line thus removing the line **(see photo 1.8)**.

On a project such as this bow, it is less important that you stay exactly on the line because the bow will be sawed apart and put back together which will make for a nice fit; however, when sawing different projects that have different colors of wood, the sawing would need to be more accurate. After removing the knot, you can saw out the rest of the bow. Just remember to plan your sawing so you don't wind up with very tiny pieces to hold on to. Try to plan your cuts so you are holding onto a larger piece of material and the good part will just drop off the main piece of material **(see photo 1.9)**.

After all the parts have been cut, the burr or tear-out on the back side should be removed before assembling the project **(see photo 1.10)**.

Checking for Fit

Before taking the paper off, it's a good idea to check the overall project to see if everything is fitting correctly. Because we cut the bow out of the same piece of wood, there shouldn't be a fit problem. If you had to use two pieces of wood for the bow, there may be some discrepancies where the two sections meet. The lines remaining on the pattern may reveal where the fit problem is. If there is not any line work evident and there is still a fit problem, you can make a mark on the part and trim it with the saw. We use a new sharp blade in the scroll saw to trim any parts.

Shaping

Before removing the paper, transfer the number from the pattern onto the back of the part **(see photo 1.11)**. When you are satisfied with the fit, remove the paper **(see photo 1.12)**. At this stage, it is a good idea

 **Lesson One**

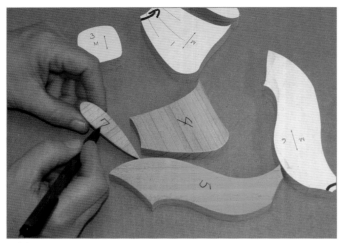

1.11

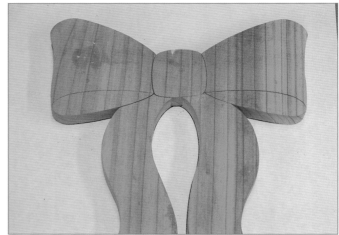

1.12

to take a minute and study the project again. I like to get a general idea of what I plan on doing. I start with the parts that would be the background, or the parts that would be the farthest from the viewer.

Here's The Plan

On the bow, the two hanging ribbons are the parts farthest from the viewer. The first parts you sand will determine how much dimension your project will have. My plan is to start with the two hanging ribbons. I'll (just for now) taper the ribbons toward the bow, sanding them down to about ¼". Then I'll sand the next step up, which is the parts that make up the backs of the bow. Next I'll sand the upper bow parts. Last I'll sand the center of the bow. With this plan in mind, I start the shaping process.

Now to actually start the shaping follow the steps below.

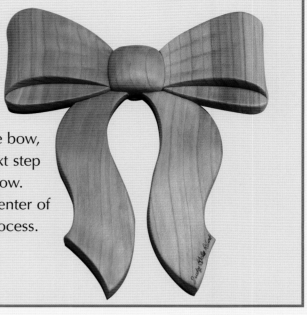

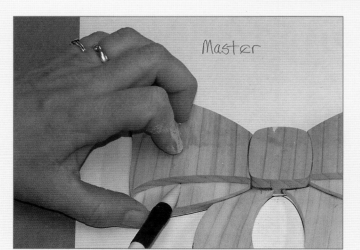

Step 1

I use a soft, flexible sander and press each piece firmly against the drum. If you don't have a soft drum sander, you can use a belt sander, hard drum sander or any other sander that will help shape the wood. The soft sander makes it easier to get flowing, smooth contours. Sand the ribbons down toward the bow, bringing it down to about a ¼". With a mechanical pencil mark where the ribbons join the lower side of the bow. These pencil lines will be a guide for you.

Step 2

Sand the two small parts under the bow down to about ½". You can mark a ½" line on the part to give you a line to sand to. On one side of the part, it will have the mark you made from the ribbons. Do not sand below these pencil lines. Many times I will hold the part with the critical pencil line facing me, so I can watch it at all times. After you have sanded the two parts down to about a ½" put them back in place and mark with a pencil where these two parts join the bow.

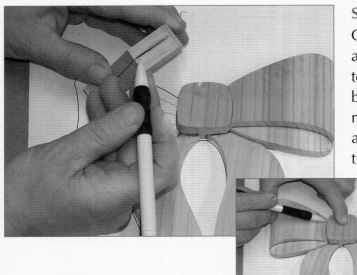

Step 3

On the two upper bow sections, mark a line about a ½" from the bottom up on the area that touches the center of the bow. Taper the upper bow parts down toward the center to your ½" mark. While you have the parts out, go ahead and round the outside edges of the bow. Mark the center of the bow using the two upper bow parts for height.

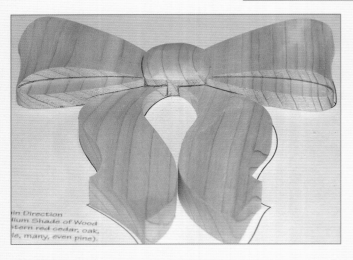

Step 4

Round the center of the bow toward the new pencil lines; then, round the center on the top and the lower part where they join the two hanging ribbons. Be sure to stay above the pencil lines that indicate the thickness of the ribbons.

Step 5

The bow is roughed in, and it's time to go back and start refining it. I'll refine the bow following the same order we used to rough it in. The hanging ribbons can use some more contouring. These are good parts to practice with on your sander. Place the sander toward the lower portion of the ribbon and sand a dip, making the ribbon look as though the lower part is flipping up. Once the shape is as desired, clean up the parts. What I mean by this is sand all that you can with the sander, sanding in the same direction as the grain. I have two drums, one with a 100/120-grit sleeve and one with a 220-grit sleeve. I sand any exposed/outside edges on all the parts as I go.

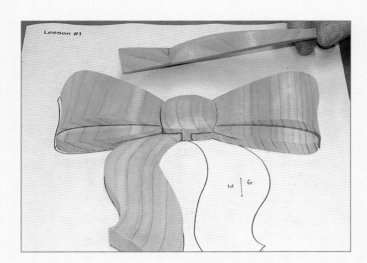

Step 6

If you alter the height of the hanging ribbons where they meet the bow, remark the new thickness line. I like to sand some curves and a dip in the ribbons to give them a softer feel.

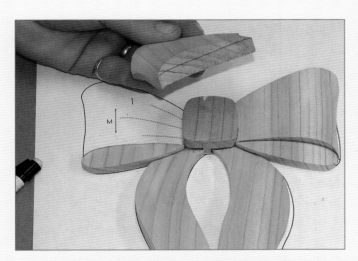

Step 7

Next work on the two upper bow sections. If you didn't round the outside edges, do that at this time. Round it almost all the way to the bottom edge of the wood. Since this is a free form piece, you can take advantage of the sides of the wood to make your project look even more dimensional. If you need make the part under the bow match the roundness, use your pencil to mark the new thickness and sand the lower bow portion to match it.

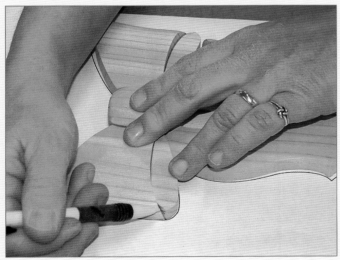

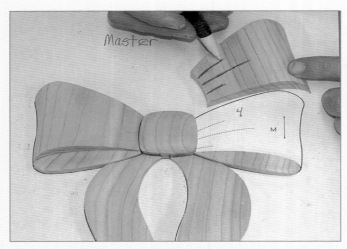

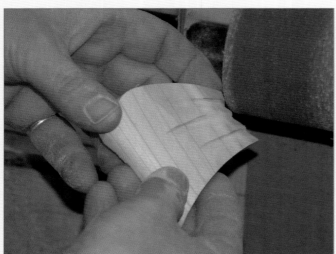

Step 8

I like to add some wrinkles/folds in the bow. Using the dashed lines as a guide, carve, burn or cut these lines for added detail. I like to carve the lines using the edge of the sander. A hand rotary tool may do the trick also. Use a pencil and mark where you want the lines. You can use carbon paper to transfer the lines from the pattern if desired. I use the edge of the drum and follow the line. Clean up any exposed edges and place the upper bow parts back.

Step 9

We rounded the upper bow portions, so we need to adjust the lower, or backside, of the bow pieces to follow the same curve. With the pencil, mark where the outer edge of the bow joins the lower/backside of the bow. Put a concave curve on the backside of the bow parts, blending it to the rounded part of the upper bow.

Step 10

The last part is the center, which is the thickest. You will have pencil marks on three of the four sides. Sand the section with the grain and once again clean up any exposed edges.

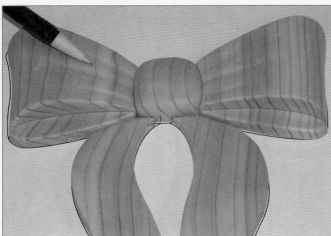

Step 11

Erase any pencil lines that may be showing and check again for any deep scratches. Lightly go over each part by hand with 180 then 220-grit sandpaper, lightly sanding all the sharp edges. You can see where the grain pattern changed where the creases were sanded. Doing details like this will add to the beauty of the overall finished project.

1.30

1.31

1.32

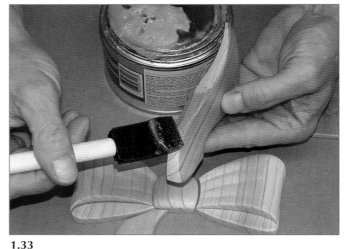

1.33

Applying the Finish

Before you begin, be sure to read and follow the manufacturer's recommendations and cautions for applying their specific finish.

There are many finishes on the market today as well as many techniques for applying them. In the beginning, we used to spray the project after it was glued to the backing, which is probably the fastest method, but we feel that it is not the best method to achieve our desired finish. Our method of choice is to use a Polyurethane wiping gel, which is applied to each part before the project is glued to the backing.

Before we begin, we clean the surface of any dust by using compressed air from our air compressor. Each part is blown off, including the edges and back. We need a few aids for applying and removing the gel. For applying the gel we use a 1" disposable foam brush. We will also need some paper towels and a piece of scrap ¼" plywood

to use as a paddle to remove the gel from the can (see photo 1.30).

After opening the can, I turn the lid over and use the paddle (see photo 1.31) to remove some gel. I place the gel on the underside of the lid and then place the lid (upside down) back on the can. If you work out of an open can there will more than likely be a skin that forms over the gel. If a skin does develop, it can be removed providing it is not too thick.

When applying the gel, be sure to use a liberal amount (see photo 1.32), especially on the first coat. Notice how the gel brings out the richness of the cedar (see photo 1.32). I apply the gel to the sanded side of the part and then apply it to all edges (see photo 1.33). We do not coat the back of the part. Notice (see photo 1.33) that my thumb is in contact with the coated side as I coat the edges. The gel is very forgiving, and where my thumb made contact, I just apply a little more gel to the spot.

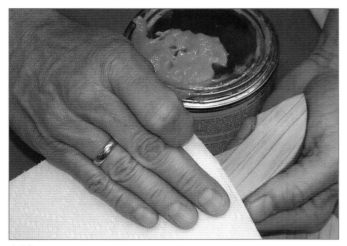

1.34

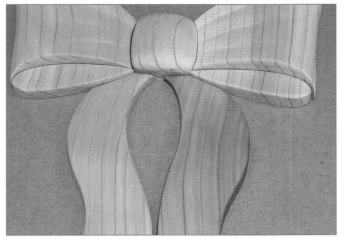

1.35

1.36

After the gel has been applied, it is ready to wipe off in about one minute. We use paper towels (a full sheet, folded into fourths) to wipe the gel off the parts **(see photo 1.34)**. Use one towel to wipe off the excess and go around the edges; then, use a fresh towel to buff the part with the grain. Normally the first towel and the buffing towel can be used for four or five parts before they need to be changed. When it's time to change the towels, the buffing towel can be used to wipe off the excess and a new towel can be used for the buffing towel.

Normally I will coat two or three pieces before I start to wipe the parts off. I wipe all of the parts and then start the process all over again until all the parts have been coated. Notice how the wood gets richer-looking after the gel has been applied **(see photo 1.35)**. We allow the first coat to dry overnight to make sure it has dried thoroughly. The second coat can be applied the same way as the first coat, except we do not coat all of the edges, only the edges that are exposed around the outside of the project. After four to six hours we will apply the third and final coat. The gel works very well with the cedar and does not raise the grain, so there is no need to sand or use steel wool between coats. The gel will raise the grain slightly on white woods like aspen and white pine, so we steel wool lightly with 0000 before applying the third coat. After the third coat has dried (in about four hours), the project can be assembled.

We have noticed in the past that a white wood like white pine or basswood will have a tendency to yellow or turn tan after applying the first coat of gel. If you would like the white parts to stay white, a coat of white gel can be applied as the first coat. We choose to use aspen as our white wood, because it will not turn yellow or tan

when the gel is applied.

Note: Some parts will have sharp inside corners, which may make it difficult to remove the gel. These areas can be blown with compressed air, which liquifies the gel. When blowing these areas, be sure to check the tops of the parts for any gel that may have run and wipe these areas immediately.

If by chance a part has been left too long before wiping, the gel will become tacky. Just apply more gel to it and wait a few seconds before you start wiping. If you want to "stain" the white wood a color, artist oil color can be added to the gel and then applied as the first coat. When doing this, be sure to do some tests on scrap pieces of wood first.

The foam brush can be wrapped in plastic wrap or a bag and can be used again for up to three days. For cleaning our hands we use a "waterless" hand cleaner like Goop first and then wash them with soap and water.

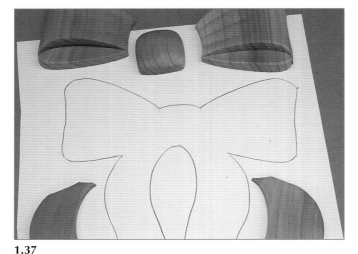

1.37

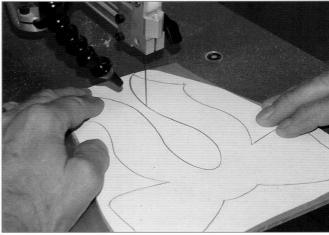

1.38

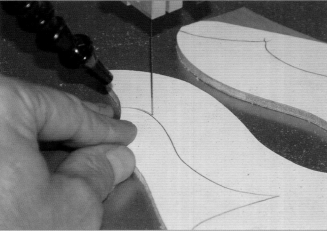

1.39

1.40

Make the Backing

After the gel has dried, you can make your backing. We use ¼" Luan plywood. I like to trace around the actual parts, rather than use the pattern (see photo 1.36). Many times I sand the edges or alter the shape from the pattern in one way or another. I trace around the project on a white piece of paper that I sprayed with a light coat of spray adhesive to keep the parts from sliding around while I draw around them (see photo 1.37). Then I use more adhesive spray and stick the paper to ¼" Luan plywood. When I saw the backing, I stay to the inside of the line (see photos 1.38 and 1.39) about ½" to ⅟₁₆". This will make the backing a little smaller than the project. We do this in order to make sure that the backing does not hang out past the project when the pieces are glued down.

After the backing is cut out, I sand the edges then stain them with a dark brown leather dye (see photo 1.40). The dye is alcohol based and dries very quickly.

Put the parts on the backing to check how they fit on the backing (see photo 1.41). We sand the back of the backing to remove most of the dye that may have run. Do not sand the front gluing surface. To help seal the entire project, we spray clear acrylic on the back and the edges of the backing.

Glue the Bow Down

On the bow I used a combination of woodworkers glue and hot melt glue to glue the pieces down. I use the hot glue to act as a clamp until the woodworkers glue dries. We have a glue gun that heats up to 400 degrees, which makes the glue very thin. If you plan on using a hot glue gun, you will need to get a gun that heats to at least 350 degrees, otherwise your parts will not lie flat against the backing. The hot glue will cool and harden before you have time to press it into place.

To glue the bow, first I check for placement on the backing, going for optimum fit. Then I carefully pick up

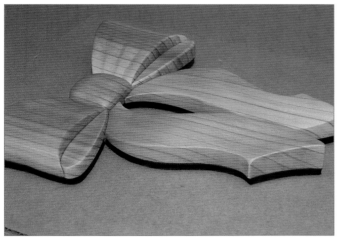

1.41

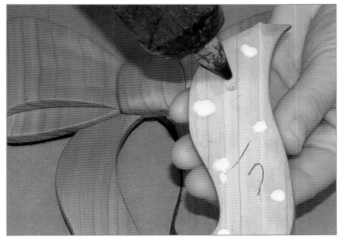

1.42

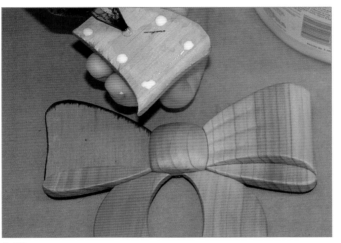

1.43

one of the parts that will help lock the project in. In this case, one of the hanging ribbons is large enough to accommodate both the hot glue and the woodworkers glue. I put small dots of the woodworkers glue down first, leaving space between for the hot glue. I check the project and get another view of its final position. I fix the plan in my mind so I can move as quickly as possible. Then I apply the hot glue and press the part firmly in place **(see photo 1.42)**. Hold it for about 15 seconds without moving it. Moving around to the other side to lock another part in place, I glued the left bow part using the same technique **(see photo 1.43)**.

With these two parts locked in place, there is not much fear of the parts moving around as you glue them down. Using just dots of the woodworkers glue will be ample glue to hold the parts. Too much glue can cause the wood to warp. Allow the glue to set before putting on the hanger.

Put on the Hanger

For pictures of the technique used, refer to the "Put on the Hanger" section in Lesson Eight.

Lesson Two

Bow and Bells

You will study your wood to take advantage of wood that varies from a light to a darker shade. Also, we will add another color of wood to learn how to make parts fit that are cut from different pieces of wood.

TOOLS:

- Scroll saw or bandsaw
- #5 reverse skip tooth blades
- Sander for contouring, (Softer is better. A pneumatic (air-inflated) sander is best, however a belt sander or disc sander will work also.)
- Carving knife or woodburner (optional)

MATERIALS:

- A medium shade of wood at least 6½"x 7½" x ¾"
- A light shade of wood at least 5"x 5" x ¾" thick
- Repositionable spray adhesive or glue stick
- At least four copies of the Bow and Bells pattern
- ¼" Luan plywood for the backing
- Woodworkers glue
- ⅜" drill bit

Pattern Preparation/Layout

Glance over the pattern. The Bow and Bells pattern has two colors of wood, and the grain direction is the same on all of the bow parts. The jingle bells with the string are a different color and have a different grain direction. This tells me I will need at least two copies of the pattern to make the bow and bells. I like to make a couple of extra copies, one for my "master" and an extra one just in case. See if you have wood that is wide enough to layout the bow and the bells in one section. If not, get an additional copy of the pattern made. Four copies should be enough if your wood is wide enough to lay out the two different colors.

Check what colors of wood are involved. On the bow there is only one color, M, a medium shade of wood. The bells are LT, a light shade (see photo 2.1). This project has more detail than the Bow in Lesson One. I like to use wood that is at least ¾" thick and has wood grains and colors that will enhance the project. If you have any wood that goes from a lighter shade to a darker shade, it would look great on the bow. Put the lighter part along the top of the bow. This will give the

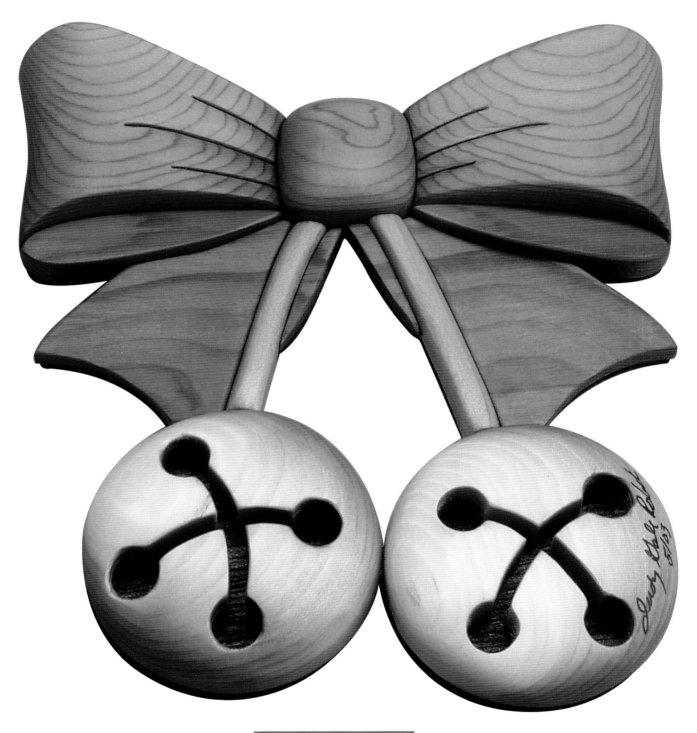

Bow and Bells

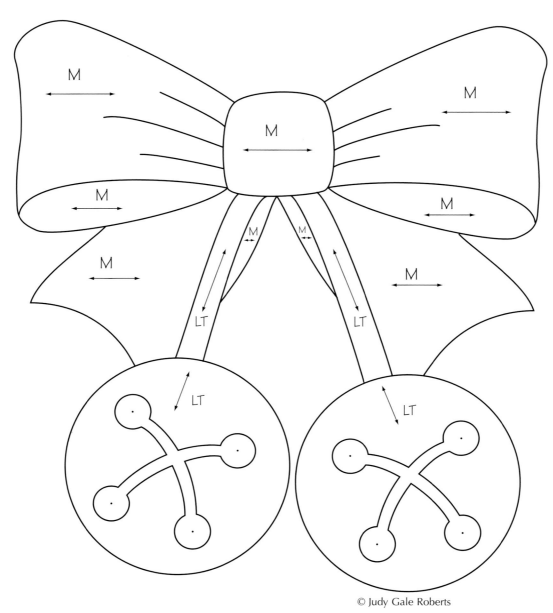

© Judy Gale Roberts

Pattern is shown actual size

⟷ ....Grain Direction
LT............Light Shade of Wood
M............Medium Shade of Wood

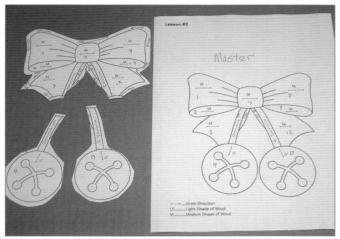

2.1

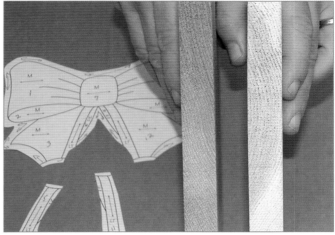

2.2

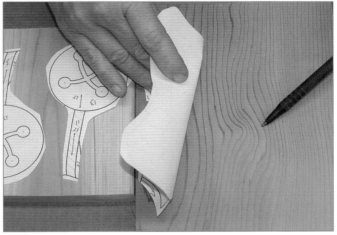

2.3

bow more depth just from the coloration of the wood. If you choose to use gradated wood for the bells, put the lighter portion on the top side of all the parts. It's amazing how much more depth your project will have. Before you glue your pattern parts onto wood with lighter shades, always check both sides of the board to see how deep the lighter shade goes. It's always sad to sand off the light part **(see photo 2.2)**. If there is some unique grain pattern on the wood I like to put it somewhere on the project to accentuate it. The wood I chose for the bow has some grain that I will use for the center of the bow **(see photo 2.3)**.

We use Western red cedar, which comes somewhat smooth on the face and both edges. We run the rough side through a planer, taking off just enough wood so the piece lies flat. Clean up both sides if needed, but try to conserve the thickness of the wood. Use whatever wood you have on hand for this project.

Label one of the pattern copies as your master. I like to number each part on the master. Next take one of the copies and trim it, giving it about a ¼" border around the line work. Cut the pattern pieces for the bow out of one copy, and use another copy for the bells. Transfer the numbers from the master onto the pattern pieces.

Now we will glue the pattern to the wood. Get your wood as dust free as possible. I use a re-stickable glue stick. It is a water-based product that works great for me. A repositionable spray adhesive will do the job also. The trick with the glue stick is to let it dry for about 20 to 30 seconds before putting it on the wood, then burnish it down for extra staying power. It's better to put too much glue than not enough. There is nothing more frustrating than cutting a critical area and the paper starts flapping. Also, I've noticed if any of the paper pattern is hanging over the wood, it will start to peel back. I trim any paper even with the edge of the board. Another thing that I like to do is mark arrows on all the outside edges. This way, when you start sawing, you can cut the outside

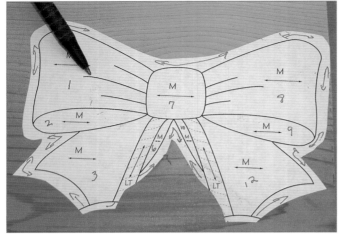

2.4

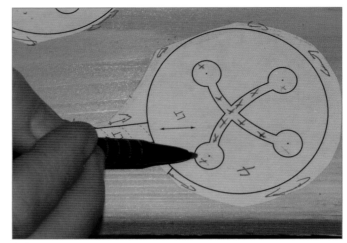

2.5

2.6

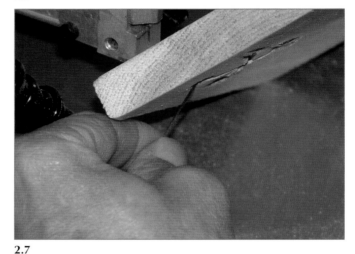

2.7

edges first. Nothing fits next to the outside parts, so you can relax a bit and get into the swing of sawing before you have to make any parts fit.

Before you start sawing out your parts, drill the ⅜" holes in the bells. It's a good idea to do any drilling before you start cutting the parts out.

Scroll Sawing

Although this bow looks similar to the first bow, it is quite different as far as the sawing goes. Several of the parts get cut apart as the first bow, but this one also has some parts that are different colors and therefore must be cut separately and then used with the other colors. This makes the sawing a little tougher, and the cuts must be more accurate.

The colors marked with an M all have the same grain direction and therefore can be cut in the same manner as the first bow; however, the parts marked with LT must be cut separately and then assembled along

with the M parts. This makes it necessary to saw more accurately in order to achieve a nice fit.

I will start sawing this bow in the same place as the first bow (starting with the knot first). You will notice that there are three solid lines running from the knot on each side **(see photo 2.4)** that just end. These lines, when drawn solid are called veins, which you cut to the end and then back out. After all the M parts have been cut, it is time to cut the LT parts.

Before cutting the LT parts, the round ends of the crosses on the bells require drilling. First, drill the ⅜" holes at the end of the crosses using the dot in the center as the starting point for the drill **(see photo 2.5)**. After the drilling **(see photo 2.6)** is complete, it is best to cut the slots before the rest of the sawing is done. This allows you to have more material to hold onto instead of waiting until all the parts have been cut out. In order to cut this area, a scroll saw (or a coping saw) must be used. To do this, I loosen the top blade holder to release the

2.8

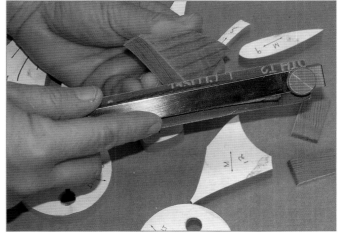

2.9

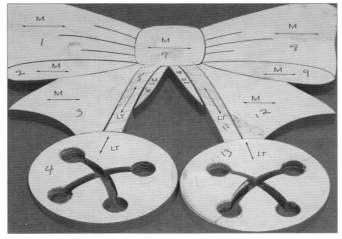

2.10

blade and thread the blade through the bottom of the part **(see photo 2.7)**; then, I tighten the top blade clamp and tension the blade. Now the crosses can be cut **(see photo 2.8)**. After cutting the first bell, the blade can be released and threaded through the second bell in the same manner as the first one and then cut. After cutting the slots, continue cutting the outside of the bells and the string. When all the parts have been cut, remove the burr from each part **(see photo 2.9)** before checking for fit.

Remember: On this project and all other Intarsia projects, the burr must be removed before checking the fit. If this is not done before checking the fit, you may get a false reading and trim some parts that may not need to be trimmed.

Checking for Fit

Before taking the paper off, it's a good idea to check the overall project to see if everything is fitting correctly. Because the bow was cut out of the same piece of wood, there shouldn't be a fit problem. If you had to use two pieces of wood for the bow, there may be some discrepancies where the two sections meet. The line work on the pattern may reveal where the fit problem is. If there is not any line work evident and there is still a fit problem, you can make a mark on the part and trim it with the saw. We use a new sharp blade in the scroll saw to trim any parts if needed.

Shaping

Before removing the paper, transfer the number from the pattern onto the back of the part. When you are satisfied with the fit, remove the paper **(see photo 2.10)**. At this stage, it is a good idea to take a minute and study the project again. I like to get a general idea of what I plan on doing. I start with the parts that make up the background, or the parts that would be the farthest from the viewer. On the bow, the two hanging ribbons are farthest from the viewer. The first parts you sand will determine how much dimension your project will have.

Here's The Plan

Start with the two hanging ribbons. I'll sand them down to about ¼" consistently off the face of the wood. When I talk about sanding down I mean taking it off the surface. The ribbons will be ¼" thick. The reasoning behind this is to make the jingle bells stand out more and to have more area to round the bells. Next I'll sand the string for the bells, then the bells. I'll do the bow next, sanding the backside of the bow then the two upper sides. Finally I'll do the center of the bow. With this plan in mind, I start the shaping process.

Now to actually start the shaping follow the step below.

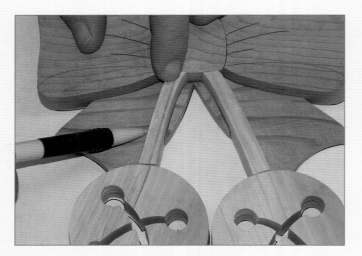

Step 1

Sand the ribbons down to about a ¼". All four pieces should be ¼" thick. With a mechanical pencil mark where the ribbons join the string/bells and the lower side of the bow. These pencil lines will be a guide for you.

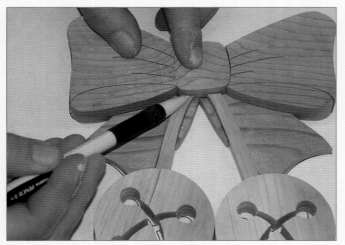

Step 2

Sand the string for the bells, staying above the pencil lines. The strings need to be thicker to give the illusion that they are on top of the ribbons. Mark where the string hits the bells and the center section of the bow.

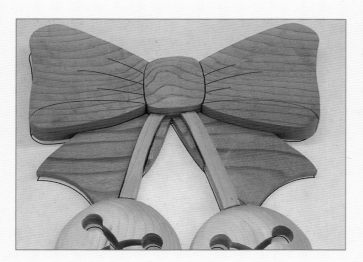

Step 3

Continue down to the bells. Sand them as round as possible, staying above your pencil lines. I hold the part so I can see my line work whenever possible. Remember: Just rough in the entire project first.

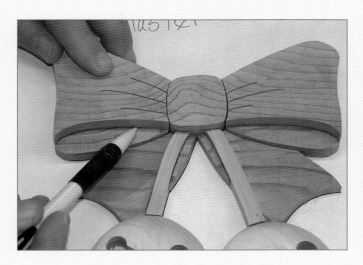

Step 4

Moving up to the backside of the bow, sand the parts down to about ½". You can mark a ½" line on the part to give you a line to sand to. On one side of the part, it will have the mark you made from the ribbons. Do not sand below these pencil lines. Many times I will hold the part with the critical pencil line facing me, so I can watch it at all times. After you have sanded the two parts down to about a ½", put them back in place and mark with a pencil where these two parts join the bow.

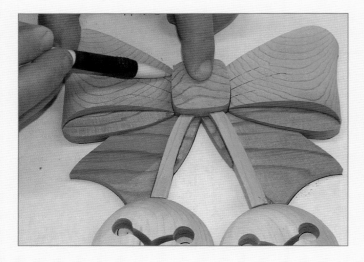

Step 5

Take the two upper bow sections and, with your pencil, mark a line about a ½" from the bottom up on the area that touches the center of the bow. Taper the upper bow parts down toward the center to your ½" mark. While you have the parts out, go ahead and round the outside edges of the bow. Put the parts back in place to mark the center of the bow using the two upper bow parts for height.

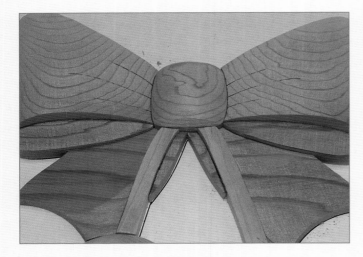

Step 6

Round the center of the bow toward the new pencil lines. Then round the top and the lower parts where they join the two hanging ribbons. Be sure to stay above the pencil lines that indicate the thickness of the ribbons.

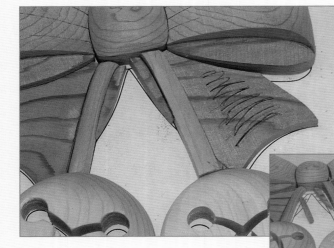

Step 7

The bow is roughed in, and it's time to go back and start refining it. To make things easy, I'll refine the project following the same order used to rough it out. To relieve some of the flatness of the ribbons, roll the outside edges on both ribbons. I make an effort not to round all the parts too heavily. Having a combination of some flatter areas against the rounded parts makes the overall project look much better. Sanding all the parts round can get somewhat monotonous. You tend to see all the parts rather than the entire picture. Once the shape is as desired, clean up the parts. What I mean by this is sand all that you can with the sander, sanding in the same direction as the grain. I have two drums, one with a 100/120-grit sleeve and one with 220-grit sleeve. I sand any exposed/outside edges on all the parts as I go. Many times I will mark with a pencil areas I want to sand down on the top side of the wood. That way when I get to the sander I know exactly where I want to remove wood. As you can see in the photo, the ribbon is very thin, close to ¼" thick.

Step 8

If you alter the height of the hanging ribbons where they meet the bow or the bells, remark the new thickness line with a pencil.

Step 9

Round the strings almost to the pencil line showing the thickness of the ribbons. Clean up any exposed edges and put the strings back in place.

Step 10

Round the bells all the way down the sides on all the exposed edges. Stay above the pencil lines where the ribbon and string touch.

Step 11

Moving back up to the bow, match the contour of the backside of the bow (backside) with the upper bow parts.

Step 12

On the upper bow parts, add more detail to the cut/fold lines on the bow by sanding the edge on both sides of the cut. This will make the cuts look more dimensional and intentional.

Step 13

If you sanded the two bow parts that join the center section, remark the center and round the center part to the line. Clean up exposed areas and the surface of all the parts as you go.

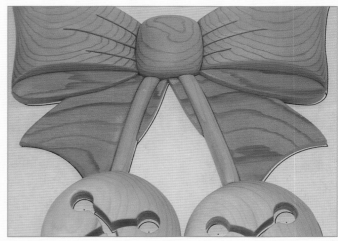

Step 14

Erase any pencil lines that may be showing and check again for any deep scratches.

2.20

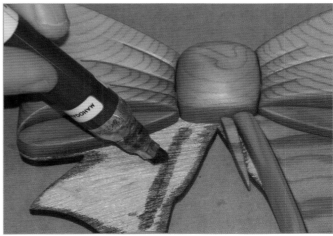

2.21

Applying the Finish

Dust or blow off all the parts. Refer to the finishing section for the Bow in Lesson One.

Make the Backing

After the gel has dried, you can make your backing from ¼" Luan plywood. (Refer to Lesson One for general instructions.) The jingle bells have large empty spaces showing to make them look more like real jingle bells. If your plywood backing is light, like mine, you may want to darken the plywood under these areas. It will look much better with a darker tone in there (see photo 2.20). Also, if you have any gaps between parts, making the plywood backing darker can make the gap less obvious (see

photo 2.21). To help seal the entire project, we spray clear acrylic on the back and the edges of the backing.

Glue the Parts Down

On the Bow and Bells I used woodworkers glue on all the smaller parts. Using just dots of glue will be ample to hold the all the parts. I glued the small parts first, then glued the bow parts. Allow the glue to set before putting on the hanger. For more details on gluing refer to the gluing section in Lesson One.

Put on the Hanger

For pictures and instructions on adding a hanger, see Lesson Eight.

Lesson Three

Whale

In this lesson you will learn to use a
"Sanding Shim" to sand sections as a unit
when you need a consistent contour.
Also, you will work with two shades of wood,
use a dowel for the eye, and add detail
using a woodburner.

TOOLS:

- Scroll saw or bandsaw
- #5 reverse skip tooth blades
- Sander for contouring, (Softer is better. A pneumatic (air-inflated) sander is best, however a belt sander or disc sander will work also.)
- Carving knife or woodburner (optional)

MATERIALS:

- A dark shade of wood at least 4" x 13" x ¾"
- A white shade of wood at least 2" x 13" x ¾" thick
- Repositionable spray adhesive or glue stick
- At least three copies of the Whale pattern
- ¼" Luan plywood for the backing and sanding shim
- ⅛" dowel for the eye
- ⅛" drill bit
- Woodworkers glue

Pattern Preparation/Layout

Glance over the pattern. The Whale has two colors of wood, and the grain direction is the same for all the white parts and for all the dark parts. These areas can be laid out as one section. This tells me I will need at least two copies of the pattern. I like to make a couple of extra copies, one for my master and an extra one just in case. Four copies should be enough to complete the project.

I like to use at least ¾" thick wood and find wood grains and colors that will enhance the project. We use Western red cedar, which comes somewhat smooth on the face and both edges. We run the rough side through a planer, taking off just enough wood so the piece lies flat. Clean up both sides if needed, but try to conserve the thickness of the wood. I use aspen for any areas I want to be white or for the lightest part of the project.

Label one of the pattern copies as your master. I like to number each part on the master. Take one of the copies and cut the W sections, giving them about a ¼" border around the line work. Use another copy to cut

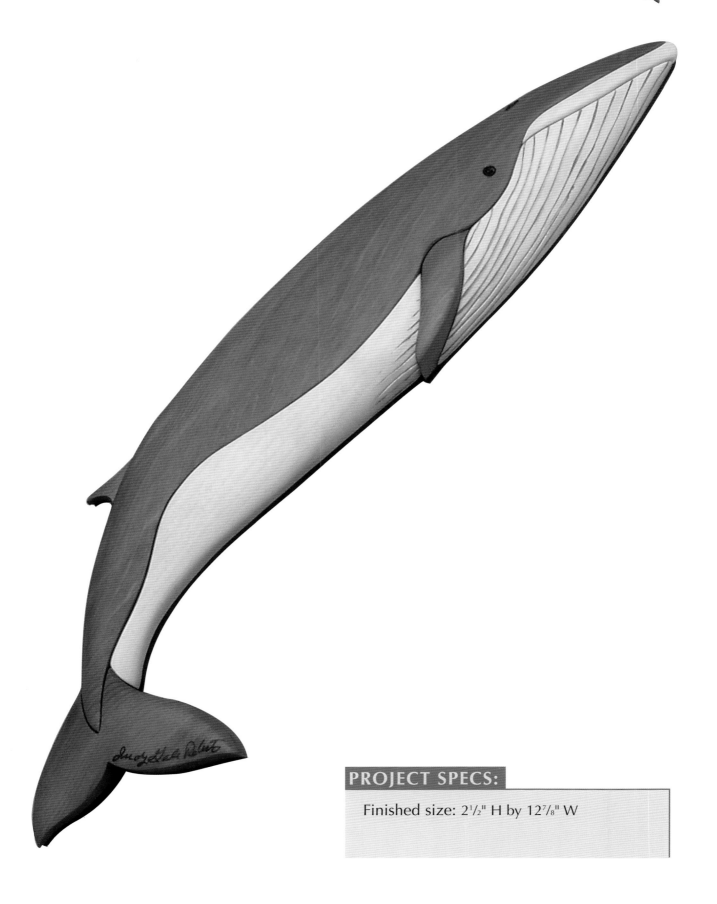

PROJECT SPECS:

Finished size: 2½" H by 12⅞" W

Whale

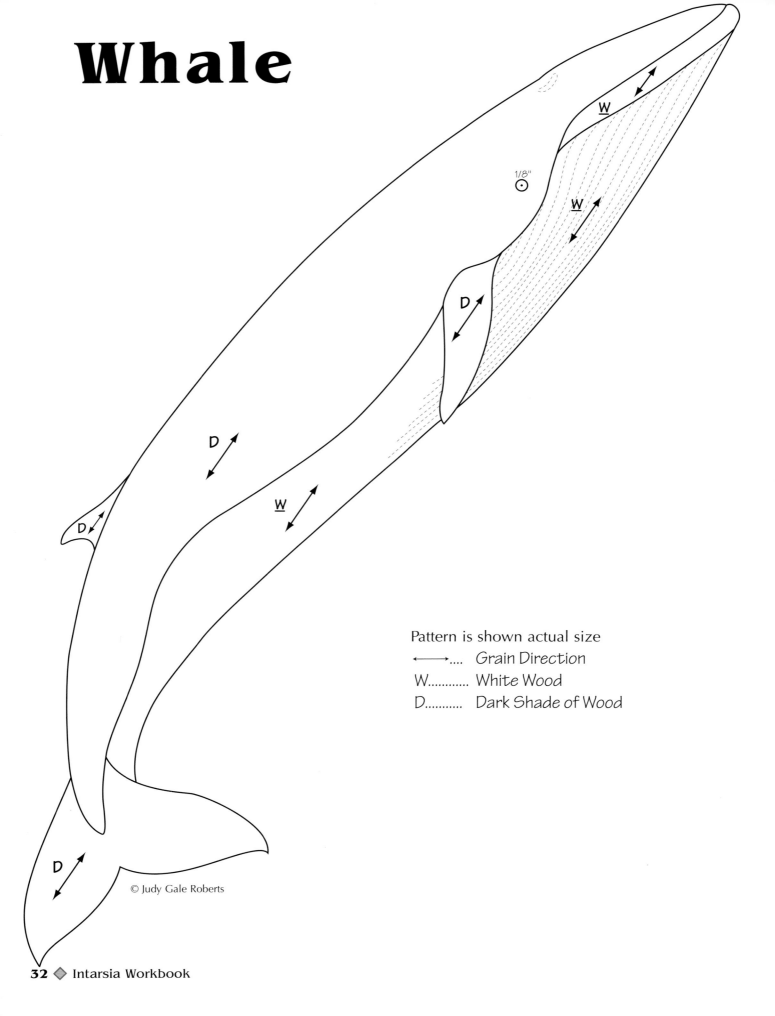

Pattern is shown actual size

←——→.... Grain Direction

W............ White Wood

D.......... Dark Shade of Wood

© Judy Gale Roberts

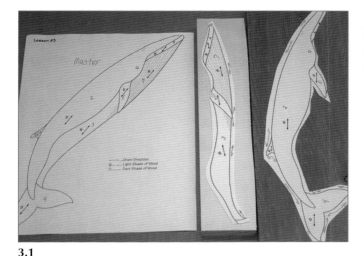

3.1

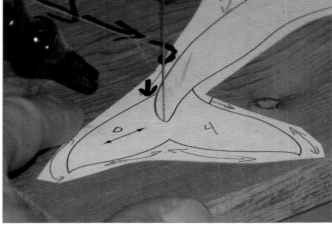

3.2

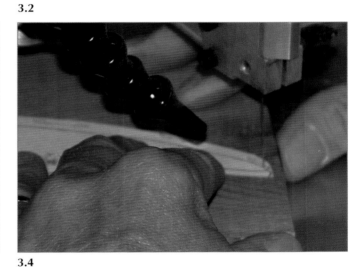

3.3

3.4

the dark parts, also leaving about ¼" border around the line work. Transfer the numbers from the master to the cut pattern pieces.

Now we will glue the pattern to the wood. Get your wood as dust free as possible. I use a re-stickable glue stick. It is a water-based product that works great for me. A repositionable spray adhesive will do the job also. It's better to put too much glue than not enough. Also, I've noticed if any of the paper pattern is hanging over the wood, it will start to peel back. I trim any paper even with the edge of the board. Another thing that I like to do is mark arrows on all the outside edges. This way, when you start sawing, you can saw the outside edges first. Nothing fits next to the outside parts, so you can relax a bit and get into the swing of sawing before you have to make any parts fit **(see photo 3.1)**.

Before you start sawing out your parts, the whale has a ⅛" hole for the eye that needs to be drilled. It's a good idea to do any drilling before you start cutting the parts out.

Scroll Sawing

Sawing the whale is a little different than sawing the bows, but it is still pretty basic. There are only two colors on the whale, a dark and a white. Notice the grain direction arrows on both colors. The grain direction is running the same on each color, and therefore, each color can be cut from the same piece of wood.

Let's start with the dark parts. Notice that the upper body, the tail and the dorsal fin, as well as the flipper, are all dark. We can cut them all from the same piece of wood. You can pretty much start anywhere you would like, but I would start from the back area between the dorsal fin and the tail. Enter the cut and proceed toward the tail where the point is **(see photo 3.2)**. Once you reach the point in the tail, back out of the cut, reverse the direction, and cut toward the head **(see photo 3.3)**. Do not follow around the dorsal fin. Instead, continue cutting along the back (we will get to the dorsal fin later) and around the head and then finally off the part **(see**

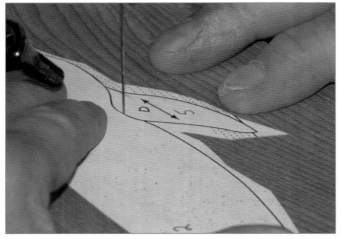

3.5

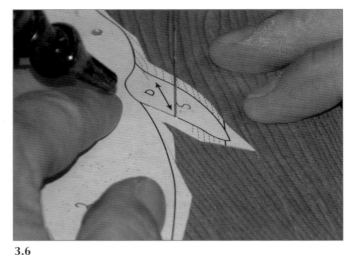

3.6

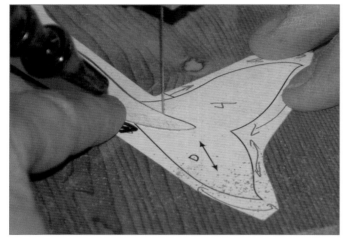

3.7

3.8

photo 3.4). Next, enter the part at the mouth area and continue cutting until you reach the fin. Go past the front part of the fin **(see photo 3.5)**, then follow the fin on its back side, **(see photo 3.6)** and then off the part. Set this section aside, then enter where the fin was on the belly of the whale and continue cutting until you get all the way into the tail **(see photo 3.7)** and join the tip of the body. The tail section will then fall away. Now you can cut the rest of the tail section and then the dorsal fin and flipper **(see photos 3.8 and 3.9)**. This will be all of the dark parts.

Now we can cut the white parts much in the same way as we did the dark parts. You could start cutting at either end, but let's just start at the upper section of the mouth and continue cutting **(see photo 3.10)** past where the fin was and onto the belly on the back side of the fin. Continue along the belly and then off the end of the part. Remember: This belly section and the dark section have to match up, so saw slowly and remove the

entire line.

Now you can start sawing at either end along the belly of the whale. This area does not have to fit against another part, so you can relax a little. If you happen to drift off the line in either direction, it is not such a big problem. After the belly section has been cut, you will be left with a long slender part that still has the mouth attached and the fin area that has to be removed **(see photo 3.11)**. You can cut either of these parts first. Once all the parts have been cut be sure to remove the burr on the backside of the project so it will sit flat.

Checking for Fit

Before taking the paper off, it's a good idea to check the overall project to see if everything is fitting correctly **(see photo 3.12)**. The whale, having the dark upper section and the white belly section, may have some fit problems between the two. Any line work on the pattern may reveal where the fit problem is. If there is not any

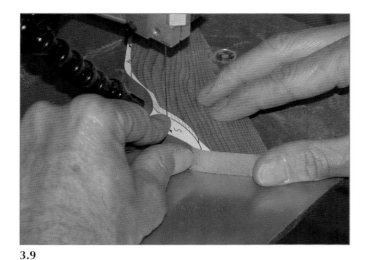

3.9

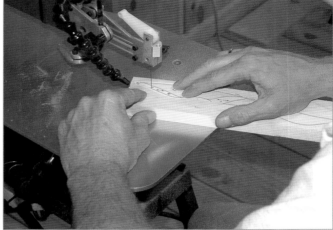

3.10

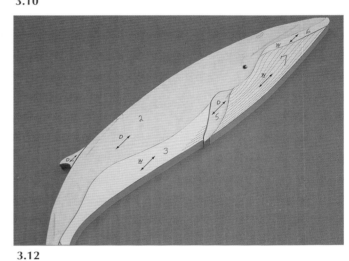

3.11

3.12

line work evident and there is still a fit problem, you can make a mark on the part and trim it with the saw. We use a new sharp blade in the scroll saw to trim any parts if needed.

Shaping

Before removing the paper, transfer the numbers from the pattern to the backs of the parts. When you are satisfied with the fit, remove the paper **(see photo 3.13)**. At this stage, it is a good idea to take a minute and study the project again. I like to get a general idea of what I plan on doing. I start with the parts that would be the background or the parts that would be the farthest from the viewer. If I am not familiar with the subject matter, I will find as many pictures as possible to aid in shaping.

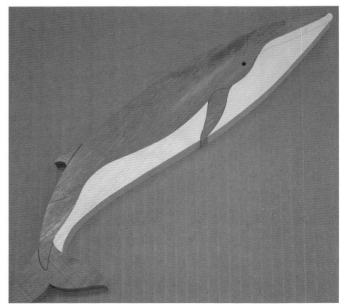

3.13

Here's The Plan

A whale is somewhat shaped like a torpedo. Whales are very streamlined to enable them to move quickly in water. I want to sand the dark and white wood together to have a consistent contour on the whale. To do this, I cut the shape of the parts I want to sand together from a scrap piece of ¼" plywood. I either use the pattern or place the parts on the ¼" plywood and draw around them **(see photo 3.14)**. Then using double-sided tape, I stick the parts together on the ¼" plywood sanding shim. Now I can sand the parts as if they were one piece of wood. In many cases this save time because there is less handling of each part. In other cases I spend more time taping up the project only to sand for about three minutes and then take it all apart to sand the rest of it individually.

At this time I will make any sanding shims I may need **(see photo 3.15)**. A sanding shim is a backing to which multiple pieces are taped. The pieces can then be sanded as one piece. Include the tail section along with the body sections.

On the whale, my plan is to start with the fin on the whale's back. This is an outside part and can be sanded down very thin if you want. I'll probably take it down to ¼". Then I will need to sand the whale's body down to about ½" thick so the side flipper will be the thickest part. With this plan in mind I start the shaping process. Remember to rough in the entire project and slowly bring it to a completion.

Now to actually start the shaping follow the steps below.

3.14

3.15

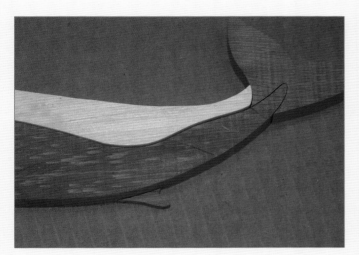

Step 1

Sand the dorsal fin down to about ¼". With a mechanical pencil mark where the fin joins the back. This pencil line will be a guide for you when you start sanding the back of the whale.

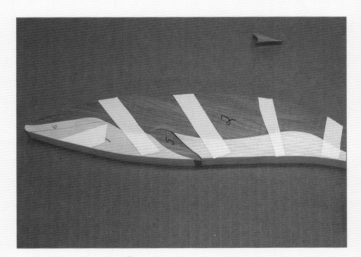

Step 2

Prepare to sand the body of the whale by turning the parts upside down. Start with the larger dark part, then place the white sections, excluding the side flipper and the white lip part (you can use it for placement, just do not put any tape on it). I prefer to place the parts upside down so I can see exactly where I need to put my tape, rather than put the tape on the sanding shim, then put the project parts on top of the shim. I like to have at least two pieces of tape on each part to hold it down to the shim. I buy the cheapest carpet tape available. You don't want a permanent bond, believe me! Another note about the tape, it is best not to leave sections taped up overnight. It seems the longer the pieces sit, the harder it is to take them apart. Dust off the parts and the backing before putting any tape on. Check to make sure your sanding shim is flat. Any warped pieces will make it almost impossible to keep your parts taped to the shim. If some parts start to come off, stop and take the time to retape it. If you try to hold it on, you will end up causing more problems in the long run.

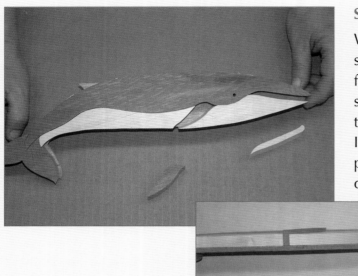

Step 3

When all the parts are secure, you are ready to start sanding the body. In order for the side flipper to be the thickest part, you will need to sand the body down to about ⅝" thick. Take this amount off the entire surface of the whale. If you just dip or sand it down where the flipper goes, it will look like the body has a deformed shape. I take the surface wood off first. If you know ahead of time the different thicknesses you will be using, you can save some sanding time and use wood already cut to different thicknesses. I usually do not take the time to preplan to that extent on smaller projects. Once the parts are close to ⅝" thick, start rounding the outside edges. Watch your pencil line for the fin on the whale's back and do not sand below that line. To sand the tail, lower both outside edges. The center where the tail joins the body will be the thickest. After you get the tail to its basic shape, remove the tail flipper. Smooth the tail along the top edges. Put it back in place and remark the white section and the dark section. Round the white belly part down below the tail line. The white section will round toward the outside edge. Next round the dark end where it joins the tail.

Remember: Just rough in these parts. Many times you will need to go back and reshape parts. Then round the tail entry part to match the flatter fin area.

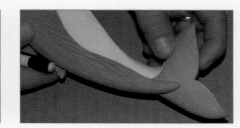

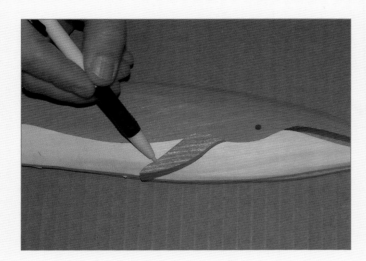

Step 4

Put the side flipper in place and mark with a pencil where the dark and white parts join. Taper the flipper toward the dark body. The flipper will be thickest at the lower edge. This will give the appearance that it is attached to the body on the side and flares out toward the bottom.

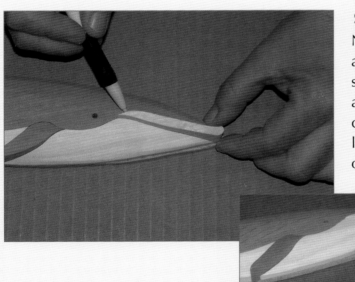

Step 5

Next put the white lip section back in place and mark around it with your pencil. Make this section just slightly thicker than the parts around it (about 1/16" thicker). Watch your pencil lines. If you do happen to sand below the line, just lower the parts around it and start over again.

Step 6

At this point the whale is roughed in. Now start to clean up each part.

Step 7

Starting with the dorsal fin on the back, sand it with the grain. To help make it look more streamlined, roll the front edge of the fin.

Step 8

With the body still taped together on the sanding shim, sand it with the grain and go over it by hand with 180 then 220-grit sandpaper. It's easier to do this while the parts are still together. Take it apart after the hand sanding.

Step 9

Clean up the tail part, sanding any exposed areas.

Step 10

Sand the side flipper and round the edge facing the front.

Step 11

Clean up the upper lip.

Step 12

Use a ⅛" dowel for the eye. Round the end of the dowel. If you are using a light color dowel it looks better if you burn it to darken it. I cut the dowel about 1½" long. It's easier to hold on to the dowel that way. I burn the exposed end, slide the dowel in from the back, mark it for length, then cut it.

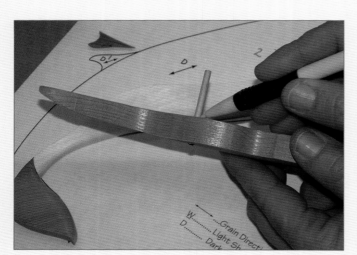

Step 13

Now for the extra detail. Mark the lines on the whale's chin/belly area, using the dashed lines on the pattern as a guide. Transfer the air hole line work at this time. We will be adding more texture to the whale. An inexpensive woodburner is very helpful for adding detail to Intarsia projects. A hand rotary tool may work also. The burning helps accentuate the lines. Clean up any exposed edges and place the white parts back in. Before burning the lines and the spot for the breathe hole, practice on some scrap wood. When you first put the burner on the wood, it has an excessive amount of heat built up. I like to put the tip of the burner on a scrap piece of wood, then start burning the good part.

Step 14

Erase any pencil lines that may be showing, and check again for any deep scratches. At this point, the project is ready to be hand sanded and de-burred.

Applying the Finish

Dust or blow off all the parts. Refer to the finishing section in Lesson One.

Make the Backing

After the gel has dried, you can cut the backing from ¼" Luan plywood. (Please refer to the instructions in Lesson One.)

Glue the Whale Down

I used hot glue on the large upper dark part of the whale then used woodworkers glue on all the rest of the parts. Using just dots of glue will be ample to hold the parts. Make sure some glue is placed on the back of the eye/dowel. For more details on gluing refer to the gluing section in Lesson One.

Put on the Hanger

For pictures and instructions on adding a hanger, see Lesson Eight.

Lesson Four

Sea Gull in Flight

You will learn how to use two sanding shims for the wing and body sections of the sea gull and some "edge taping." Also, there are four shades of wood used to make the sea gull.

Pattern Preparation/Layout

Glance over the pattern. The Sea Gull has four colors of wood. The grain direction goes many ways. I like to make a game of getting as many good parts out of a pattern using the least amount of patterns possible. When you cut up your pattern to get the complete part, you waste the other portions of the pattern. A good way to get used to this is to use a pencil and map out your cuts before actually cutting up your pattern. You can make the sea gull with three copies: two for the pattern pieces and one for your master. But it's good to have an extra one just in case. Four copies should be plenty to complete the project.

I like to use at least ¾" thick wood and find wood grains/colors that will enhance the project. We use Western red cedar, which comes somewhat smooth on the face and both edges. We run the rough side through a planer, taking off just enough wood so the piece lies flat. Clean up both sides if needed, but try to conserve the thickness of the wood. I use aspen for any areas I want to be white or for the lightest part of the project. Use whatever wood you have on hand for this project.

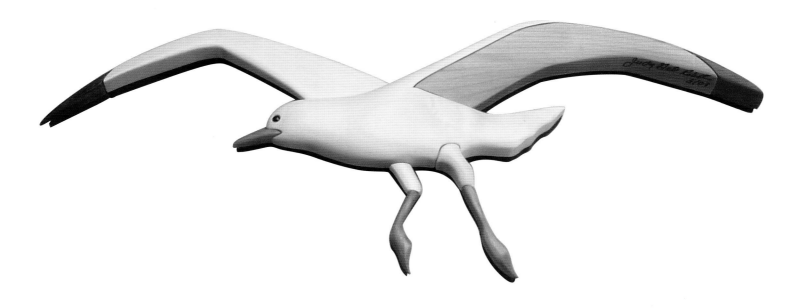

PROJECT SPECS:

Finished size: 4³/₈" H by 11¹¹/₁₆" W

Sea Gull in Flight

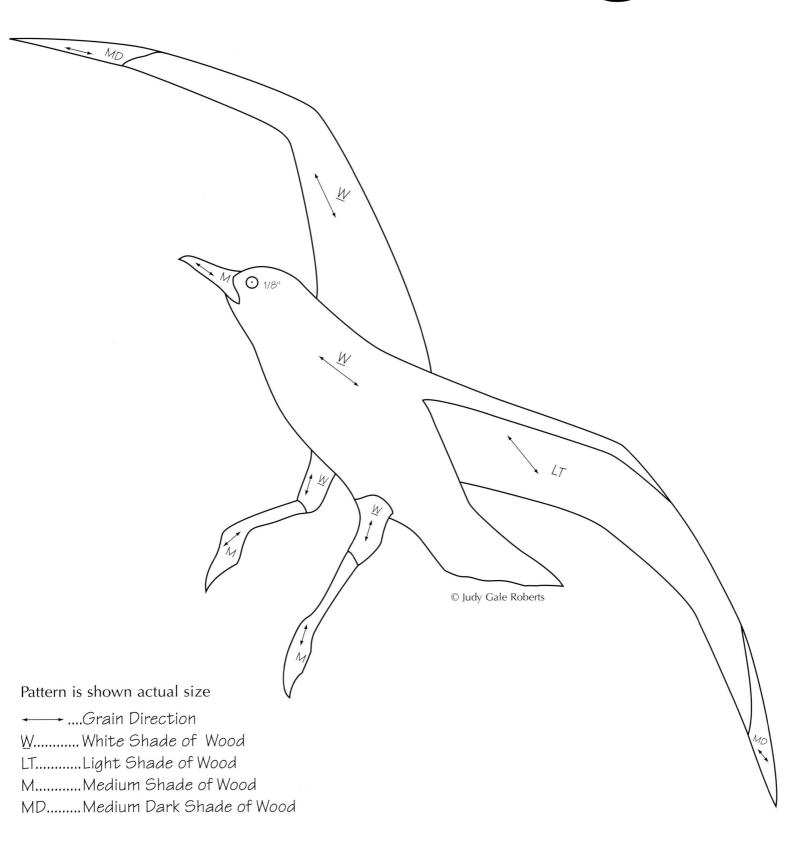

© Judy Gale Roberts

Pattern is shown actual size

⟷ ....Grain Direction

W............ White Shade of Wood

LT............Light Shade of Wood

M............Medium Shade of Wood

MD........Medium Dark Shade of Wood

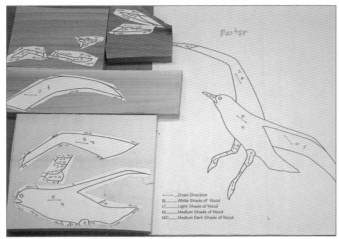
4.1

4.2

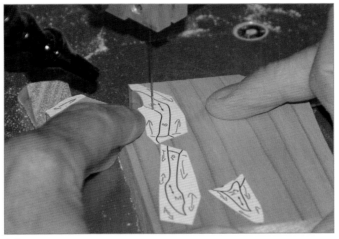
4.3

Label one of the pattern copies as your master. I like to number each section on the master. Take one of the copies and cut the body W section, giving it about a ¼" border around the line work. Then cut the two M leg parts and the two MD wing tips, giving those pattern pieces the same ¼" border. At this point there is nothing usable on the pattern. Take another copy and cut the W background wing section, the LT underwing section and the two W leg sections.

Now glue the patterns to the wood. Get your wood as dust free as possible. I use a re-stickable glue stick. It is a water-based product that works great for me. A repositionable spray adhesive will do the job also. Another thing that I like to do is mark arrows on all the outside edges. This way, when you start sawing, you can saw the outside edges first. Nothing fits next to the outside parts, so you can relax a bit and get into the swing of sawing before you have to make any parts fit (see photo 4.1).

Before you start sawing out your parts, the sea gull

has a ⅛" hole for the eye that needs to be drilled. It's a good idea to do any drilling before you start cutting the parts out.

Scroll Sawing

Once again, before beginning to saw, be sure to remove the burr on the bottom of the wood. Many times throughout the day I will check to see that my cuts are square to the bottom of the parts. This is important when cutting parts from different colors of wood (see photo 4.2).

I like to cut my woods by colors. I try to cut the light pieces, then the medium pieces and then the dark pieces. I cut the white parts last.

The feet are pretty easy to cut As you can see by the arrows (see photo 4.3) on either side of the leg, they do not have to fit another part, so if you miss the line a little it does not make any difference. Only the top part of

4.4

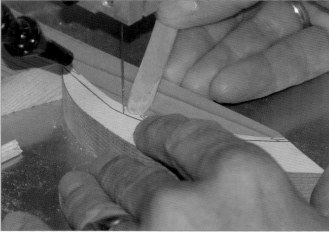

4.5

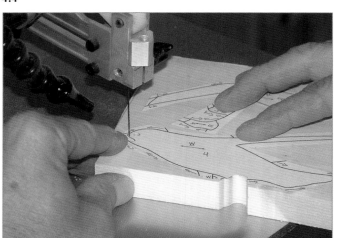

4.6

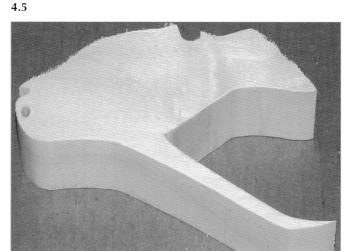

4.7

the leg has to fit. Be sure to plan your cut carefully so you do not end up with a very small part to hold onto. Try to plan your cut so the last cut you make will just drop the leg off the larger part. You can cut both legs and then the beak as shown **(see photo 4.4)**.

Another tool I have with me at all times is a wooden craft stick. In case the pattern starts to flap a little while sawing, I use the stick to hold the paper down until I can finish the cut **(see photo 4.5)**.

After all the colored parts are sawn, I will cut the "white" wood. We use aspen. It cuts differently than the cedar, so that is why I save it until last. Be sure to drill any holes, like the eye, before you start sawing **(see photo 4.6)**. I will also change to a more aggressive blade to cut the aspen better. Once all the parts have been cut, be sure to remove the burr on the bottom before checking for fit **(see photo 4.7)**.

Checking for Fit

Before taking the paper off, it's a good idea to check the overall project to see if everything is fitting correctly. Because we cut parts from many different pieces of wood there is more of a chance to have fit problems. The line work on the pattern may reveal where the fit problem is. If there is not any line work evident and there is still a fit problem, you can make a mark on the part and trim it with the saw. We use a new sharp blade in the scroll saw to trim any parts if needed.

Shaping

Before removing the paper, transfer the number from the pattern to the back of the part. When you are satisfied with the fit, remove the paper. At this stage, it is a good idea to take a minute and study the project again. I like to get a general idea of what I plan on doing. I start with the parts that make up the background, or

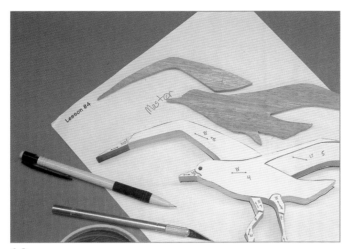

4.8

the parts that would be the farthest from the viewer. If I am not familiar with the subject matter, I find as many pictures as possible to aid in shaping.

I use sanding shims for the sea gull to sand areas consistently, and I make those now. Either use the pattern or trace around the parts to make the shim. The shim will have the beak, white body part, the light section under the wing and the medium dark tip on the wing **(see photo 4.8)**. A second shim will hold the other white part of the wing and the medium dark end piece together for sanding. Using double-sided tape, I stick the parts together on the sanding ¼" plywood shim. Now I can sand the parts as if they were one piece of wood.

Here's The Plan

On the sea gull, my plan is
to start with the leg on the left, since it is in the
background. I'll take it down to about ¼" where it joins the
body. The leg in the foreground will have to be sanded with
the body. Then I'll sand the body as a unit. Remember to
rough in the entire project and slowly bring it to a completion.

Now to actually start the shaping follow the steps below.

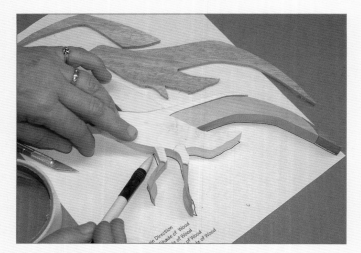

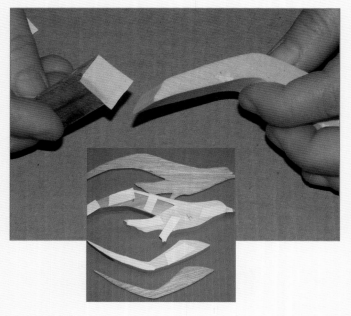

Step 1

With a mechanical pencil, mark where the left
white leg section joins the body. It helps to
know the placement and the shape of the part
where the two join. Don't guess where it goes.

Step 2

Prepare to tape both the wing and the body sections of the sea gull. I place the parts upside-
down so I can see exactly where I need to put
my tape, rather than putting tape on the sanding
shim, then putting the parts on top of the shim.
Use at least two pieces of tape on each part to
hold it down to the shim. Put tape between the
joint of the white and the medium dark parts of
the left and right wing tips. Edge-taping parts as
thin as these will help to hold them to the shim.
Dust off the parts and the backing before putting
any tape on. Remember, check to make sure
your sanding shim is flat. Any warped pieces will
make it almost impossible to keep your parts
taped to the shim. If some parts start to come off,
stop and take the time to re-tape them. The easi-
est way to remove the paper part of the double-
sided tape is to put the point of the knife blade
barely under the paper, then pull back (**see photo
4.12**). This is much easier than trying to separate
the paper at the edge of the tape.

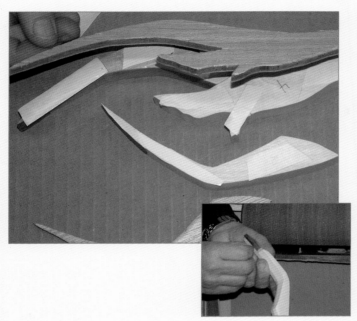

Step 3

Carefully place the sanding shim on top of the taped parts), you want to make sure all the parts are supported by the sanding shim. When all the parts are secure, you are ready to start sanding the left wing. Taper the white part down about ¼" toward the body. Take the rest of the wing down to about ½" thick. Next taper from the bend in the wing down toward the medium dark part. When you are sanding this wing section, it is best to hold the taped assembly with the dark part on the upper side. The larger white part will help support the small medium dark part to keep it in place. The high point will be the bend in the wing. Leave the left wing taped up for now.

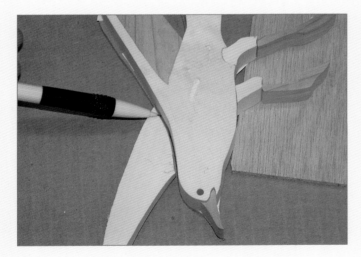

Step 4

Get ready to sand the body/wing section. Put the left wing (still taped to the shim) where it belongs against the upper body. Mark with a pencil where these two sections join. When you sand this area of the head and body stay above this pencil line.

Step 5

Use a scrap piece of ¼" plywood to raise the legs the same height as the parts with the sanding shims. Sand the left leg down to about ¼" (both the white and medium pieces). You can leave the foot part a little thicker. Mark where the left leg joins the lower body. When sanding the body section, stay above this pencil line.

Step 6

With all the outer parts sanded, we are ready to sand the body. First sand the upper right leg where it joins the body. You could sand the upper leg and body individually; however, keeping them together at this time will keep you from sanding too much off where the two join. Sand the area down to about ½", then take the white upper leg part off the sanding shim. When sanding around this area stay away from that part. Next rough in the head and beak. Round the head, tapering it down toward the beak and continuing the taper to the end of the beak. Moving now to the wing on the right, blend the white and the light woods together. Round along the top edge of the wing. Next sand the lower side of the wing, tapering it down toward the body. Get where you can with the sander while the parts are taped together, because most of it will get sanded again when we take it apart. The body is close to being roughed in. Put the left wing in place to check on how the overall project is looking. Mark the left leg. You will need to find some scrap ¼" plywood to place under the legs to keep everything the right thickness. Mark with a pencil where the white and medium sections meet. Taper the medium leg part down to the pencil line you just made. If you have sanded too much wood away around the head area, you may need to sand the left wing down some more. I mark on the face of the wood the areas that need to be sanded. If everything looks correct, take all of the parts off the sanding shim except the light and medium-dark parts of the right wing.

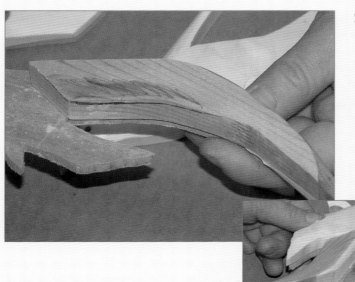

Step 7

Taper the lower portion of the LT wing part down toward the lower portion of the body. I like to mark the face of the wood to know exactly where I want to remove material before I start sanding. Then put it back together and see if there is a difference. We are trying to make the wing look as though it is tucked in behind the body.

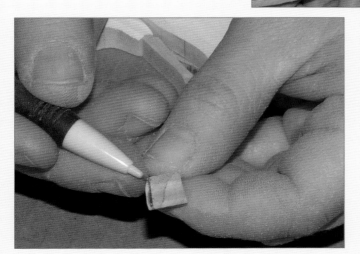

Step 8

Sand the beak down about 1/16", then put it back in place and mark the head section where the two parts join. Round the head section down to the pencil line.

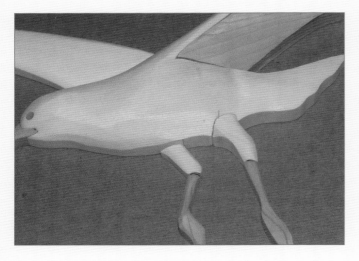

Step 9

To give the left leg more detail, taper the white part down a little toward the medium foot piece. I will sand a bend in the leg. After the taper, round it toward the outside edges. Next taper the medium leg to meet the white part. Round the upper leg section of the medium part. To give the foot a bird-like feel, sand the pointed part down toward the point. Do the same for the leg in the foreground.

Step 10

There's not much more to do to the left wing, just soften the outside edges and sand the parts with the grain.

Step 11

The last area to sand more is the tail. Taper the tail toward the outside edge.

Step 12

Last but not least is the eye. Use a ⅛" dowel for the eye. Round the end of the dowel. If you are using a light colored dowel, try darkening it with a woodburner. Slide the dowel in from the back and mark the cut-off point with a pencil line. I like to glue the dowel in at this time to keep from losing it.

Step 13

Erase any pencil lines that may be showing. Check again for any deep scratches. Hand sand where needed.

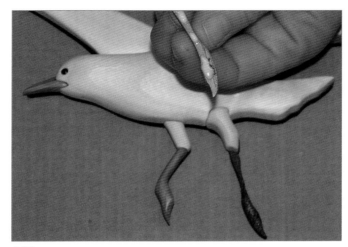

4.24

Applying the Finish

Dust or blow off all the parts, then apply the finish. (Please refer to the finish section in Lesson One.)

Make the Backing

After the gel has dried, cut the backing from ¼" Luan plywood. (Please refer to the instructions in Lesson One.)

Glue the Sea Gull Down

On the Sea Gull, I use woodworkers glue on all the smaller parts. Using just dots of glue will suffice to hold the small parts. I glue the small parts and allow them time to dry **(see photo 4.24)**. Then I use hot glue on the longer wing parts of the gull. I use both woodworkers glue and hot glue. Put the woodworkers glue first, leaving space for the hot glue. Be careful if using both types of glue, because the woodworkers glue can cool the hot glue too fast. Allow the glue to set before putting on the hanger. For more details on gluing, refer to the gluing section in Lesson One.

Put on the Hanger

For pictures and instructions on adding a hanger, see Lesson Eight.

Sea Gull Landing

You will learn how to use two sanding shims for the wing and body sections of the sea gull. Also, there are four shades of wood used to make the sea gull.

- Scroll saw or bandsaw
- #5 reverse skip tooth blades
- Sander for contouring, (Softer is better. A pneumatic (air-inflated) sander is best, however a belt sander or disc sander will work also.)
- Carving knife or woodburner (optional)

MATERIALS:

- A white shade of wood at least 5" x 9" x ¾"
- A light shade of wood at least 2"x 5" x ¾"
- A medium shade of wood at least 2" x 3" x ¾"
- A medium dark shade of wood at least 4" x 4" x ¾"
- Repositionable spray adhesive or glue stick
- At least four copies of the Sea Gull pattern
- ¼" Luan plywood for the backing and sanding shim
- ⅛" dowel for the eye
- ⅛" drill bit
- Woodworkers glue

Pattern Preparation/Layout

Glance over the pattern. The Sea Gull has four colors of wood. The grain direction goes all different ways. You can make the sea gull with three copies: two for the pattern pieces and one for your master. Then it's good to have one extra just in case. Also, some clear tape is handy in case you accidentally cut a part in two pieces. Four copies should be enough to complete the project.

I use at least ¾" thick wood and find wood grains/colors that will enhance the project.

We use Western red cedar, which comes somewhat smooth on the face and both edges. We run the rough side through a planer, taking off just enough wood so the piece lies flat. Clean up both sides if needed, but try to conserve the thickness of the wood. I use aspen for any areas I want to be white or for the lightest part of the project. Use whatever wood you have on hand for this project.

Label one of the pattern copies as your master. I like to number each part on the master. Take one of the copies and cut out the white body part including the

PROJECT SPECS:

Finished size: 10¼" H by 5" W

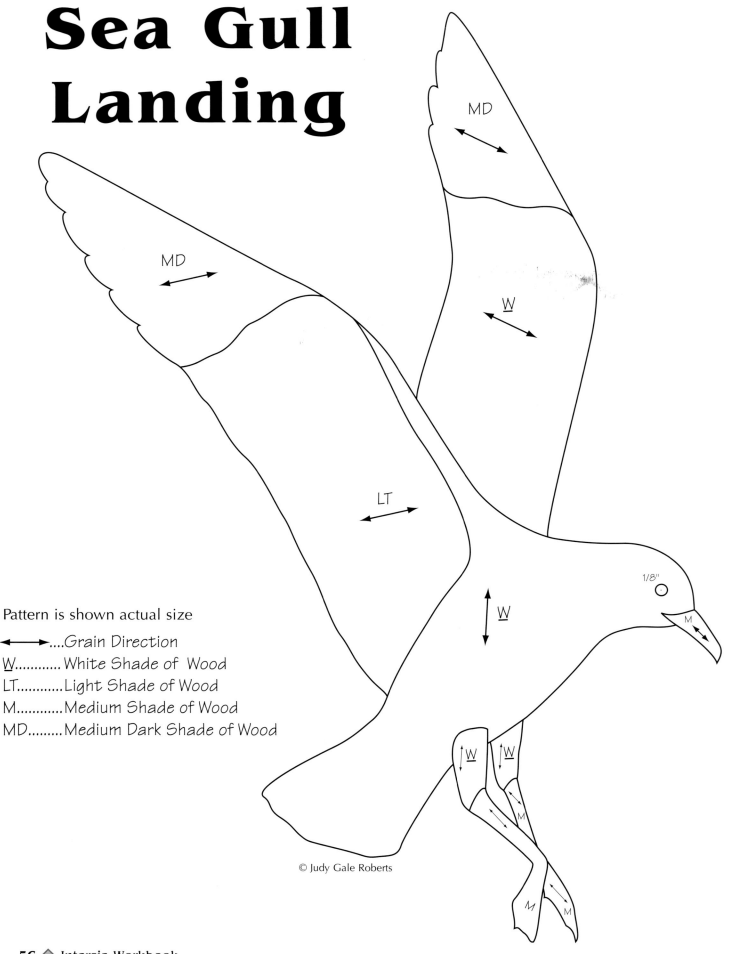

Sea Gull Landing

Pattern is shown actual size

←——————→....Grain Direction

W............White Shade of Wood

LT............Light Shade of Wood

M............Medium Shade of Wood

MD........Medium Dark Shade of Wood

© Judy Gale Roberts

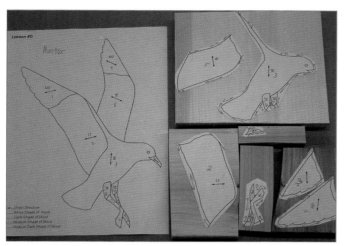

5.1

5.2

white leg parts (the color and grain direction is the same so they can be laid out together). Trim it, giving it about ¼" border around the line work. Next cut the two medium dark wing tips. At this point, you will need another copy to cut the rest of the parts. From a second copy, cut the light wing part, the white part on the right wing, the beak, and the three medium feet sections. Transfer the numbers from the master to the pattern pieces.

Next get ready to glue the pattern to the wood. Get your wood as dust free as possible. I use a re-stickable glue stick. It is a water-based product that works great for me. A repositionable spray adhesive will do the job also. I trim any paper even with the edge of the board. Another thing that I like to do is mark arrows on all the outside edges. This way, when you start sawing, you can saw the outside edges first. Nothing fits next to the outside parts, so you can relax a bit and get into the swing of sawing before you have to make any parts fit **(see photo 5.1)**.

Before you start sawing out your parts, the sea gull has a ⅛" hole for the eye that needs to be drilled. It's a good idea to do any drilling before you start cutting the parts out.

Scroll Sawing

The procedures for sawing this sea gull pattern are almost the same as those in the previous lesson. Refer to the sawing directions for Sea Gull in Flight if needed.

Checking for Fit

Before taking the paper off, it's a good idea to check the overall project to see if everything is fitting correctly. The line work on the pattern may reveal where the fit problem is. If there is not any line work evident and there is still a fit problem, you can make a mark on the part and trim it with the saw. We use a new sharp blade in the scroll saw to trim any parts if needed.

Shaping

Before removing the paper, transfer the number from the pattern to the back of the part. When you are satisfied with the fit, remove the paper. At this stage, it is a good idea to take a minute and study the project again. I like to get a general idea of what I plan on doing at this point. Take note of the wood tones used. I had some wood that went from a medium-light shade to a light shade and used it to create a shadow-like effect where the wings join the body **(see photo 5.2)**.

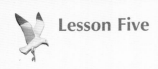

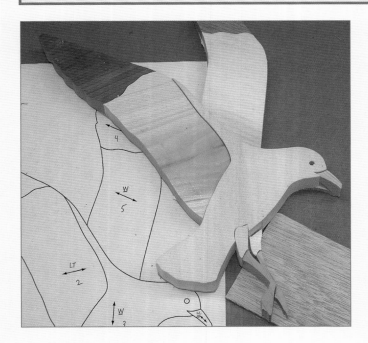

Here's The Plan

I start with the parts that make up the background, or those
that would be farthest from the viewer. If I am not familiar
with the subject matter, I will find as many pictures as possible
to aid in shaping. I use two sanding shims for the sea gull, to
sand areas consistently. Either use the pattern or trace around the
parts to make the shim. The shim will support the beak, the white
body part, the light section under the wing and the medium-dark tip
on the wing. A second shim will hold the other white part of the
wing and the medium-dark end piece together **(see photo 5.2)**.
Using double-sided tape, I stick the parts together on the ¼"
plywood shim. Now I can sand the parts as if they were one
piece of wood. At this time, I will go ahead and make any
sanding shims I may need. I'll start with the leg on the right, since
it is in the background. I'll take it down to about ¼" where it joins the body.
Next sand the wing on the right, tapering the white part down to about ¼"
toward the body. Then I'll sand the body parts together as a unit also.
Remember to rough in the entire project and slowly bring it to a completion.

Now to actually start the shaping follow the steps below.

Step 1

Tape all the parts to the sanding shims. I place
the parts upside-down, so I can see exactly
where I need to put my tape, rather than putting
tape on the shim and then putting the parts on
top of the shim. Put at least two pieces of tape
on each part to hold it down to the shim. Dust
off the parts and the backing first. Make sure
your sanding shim is flat. Any warped pieces
will make it almost impossible to keep your
parts taped to the shim. Use a scrap piece of ¼"
plywood to temporally raise the leg parts so they
will be on the same level as the body on the
sanding shim. Sand the white part of the right
leg down to about a ¼". Mark where the white
section joins the body and the medium leg/foot
parts. Sand the medium leg part next. Sand the
entire right leg down to about a ¼" thickness.
The white section and medium section are
behind the left leg, which is in the foreground.

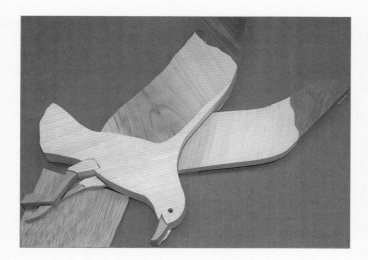

Step 2

Now you are ready to start sanding the right wing. Taper the white part down toward the body. Bring it down to about ¼" thick. In order to round the body of the sea gull you will need to remove at least ½" off the top of the white wing section. Take the rest of the wing down to about ½" thick. Next taper from the bend in the wing starting where the white and medium dark parts join down toward outer wing edge. Leave the right wing taped up for now.

Step 3

Get ready to sand the body/wing section. Put the right wing (still taped to the shim) where it belongs against the upper body. Mark with a pencil where these two sections join. When you sand this area of the body stay above this pencil line. Also note where the right leg joins the lower body, and stay above this pencil line also.

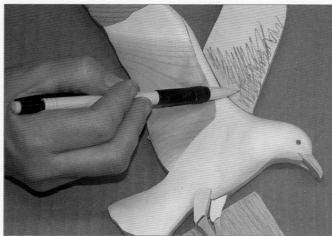

Step 4

With all the parts taped securely, sand the left leg where it joins the body (the white part). Rough in around the head and beak. Round the head, tapering it down toward the beak and continuing the taper to the end of the beak. Moving now to the wing on the left, blend the white and the light woods together. Round along the top edge of the wing. Next sand the lower side of the wing, tapering it down toward the body. Sand where you can, because most of it will get sanded when we take it apart. Taper the tail area to about ½" thick. The head around the eye area will be the thickest part. The body is close to being roughed in. Put the right wing in place to check on how the overall project is looking. If you have sanded away too much of the thickness around the head area, you may need to sand the right wing down some more. Put the left leg back in place and mark with a pencil where the body joins the leg. Lower the leg almost to the pencil line, then round the edges.

Step 5

At this point the sea gull is roughed in. Remember to use scrap ¼" plywood to keep everything the same thickness (until you take the gull parts off the sanding shims). Make a little definition between the head and body by lowering the neck area. I'll mark the face of the wood to give myself an indication where to sand once I get to the sander.

Step 6

Round the right leg toward the outside edges. To give the foot a bird-like feel sand the pointed part down toward the point. Do the same for the leg in the foreground.

Step 7

There's not much more to do to the right wing. Just soften the outside edges and sand the parts with the grain.

Step 8

Now let's start on the main part of the sea gull. Start with the light wing part first. Take the white portion of the gull off the sanding shim. Taper the light part down toward the tail. Put the light part back in place and use the pencil to mark where the light piece joins the body. When you round this section of the body you will want to stay above this pencil line.

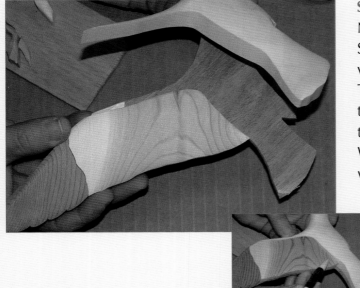

Step 9

Next finish up sanding the left leg. Sand the medium leg/foot part down to the line so it matches the white body part. Round the leg portion of the medium leg/foot part. Then taper the point of the foot down toward the bottom. Watch the pencil lines showing the thickness of the right leg. You want to stay above those lines. The left leg is in the foreground, so it should be thicker than the right leg.

Step 10

Moving around the sea gull, let's work on the face. Take the beak out and sand it down about $\frac{1}{16}$". Then mark the face area and roll the face down to the pencil line (same as the sea gull in Lesson Four).

Step 11

The last area to sand more is the tail. Taper the tail toward the outside edge.

Step 12

Last but not least is the eye. Use a $\frac{1}{8}$" dowel for the eye. If you are using a light-colored dowel, round it first, then burn the exposed area. Slide the dowel in from the back and mark the cut-off point with a pencil. I like to glue the dowel in at this time to keep from losing it.

Step 13

Erase any pencil lines that may be showing. Check again for any deep scratches and hand sand where needed.

Applying the Finish

Dust or blow off all the parts, then apply the finish. (Please refer to the finishing section in Lesson One.)

Make the Backing

After the gel has dried, make the backing from ¼" plywood. (Please refer to the instructions in Lesson One.)

Glue the Sea Gull Down

On the Sea Gull, I use woodworkers glue on all the smaller parts. Using just dots of glue will suffice to hold the small parts. I glue the small parts and allow them time to dry. The leg parts are so small that it is hard to keep them in place. Gluing them first will ensure they will be glued in the correct place. Then I use hot glue on the longer wing parts of the gull. I use both woodworkers glue and hot glue. Put the woodworkers glue first, leaving space for the hot glue. Be careful if using both types of glue, because the woodworkers glue can cool the hot glue too fast. Allow the glue to set before putting on the hanger. (For more details on gluing refer to the gluing section in Lesson One.)

Put on the Hanger

For pictures and instructions on adding a hanger, see Lesson Eight.

Chicken Pair

There are some intricate cuts to practice along with learning about using shims to raise parts, and you will get some more practice using sanding shims.

TOOLS:

- Scroll saw or bandsaw
- #5 reverse skip tooth blades
- Sander for contouring, (Softer is better. A pneumatic (air-inflated) sander is best, however a belt sander or disc sander will work also.)
- Carving knife or woodburner (optional)

MATERIALS:

- A white shade of wood at least 6" x 10" x ¾"
- A medium shade of wood at least 5" x 5" x ¾"
- A medium dark shade of wood at least 2" x 3" x ¾"
- Repositionable spray adhesive or glue stick
- At least four copies of the Chicken Pair pattern
- ¼" Luan plywood for the backing and sanding shim
- ⅛" and ¼" dowels for the eye
- ⅛" and ¼" drill bits
- Woodworkers glue

Pattern Preparation/Layout

Glance over the pattern. The Chicken Pair has three colors of wood. The grain direction goes different directions. To make the chickens, you will need three copies of the pattern: two for the pattern pieces and one for your master. Then it's good to have one extra just in case. Also, some clear tape is handy in case you cut a good part in two. Four copies should be enough to complete the project.

I use at least ¾" thick wood and find wood grains/colors that will enhance the project.

We use Western red cedar, which comes somewhat smooth on the face and both edges. We run the rough side through a planer, taking off just enough wood so the piece lies flat. Clean up both sides if needed, but try to conserve the thickness of the wood. I use aspen for any areas I want to be white or for the lightest part of the project. Use whatever wood you have on hand for this project.

Label one of the pattern copies as your master. I like to number each part on the master. Next take one of the copies and cut the white parts of both chickens,

PROJECT SPECS:

Finished size: Hen—7$\frac{1}{2}$" H by 7$\frac{1}{16}$" W
Chick—3$\frac{3}{8}$" H by 2$\frac{1}{8}$" W

Chicken Pair

© Judy Gale Roberts

Pattern is shown actual size

←——→ ....Grain Direction

W............ White Shade of Wood

M............ Medium Shade of Wood

MD........ Medium Dark Shade of Wood

R............ Raise this section 1/4"

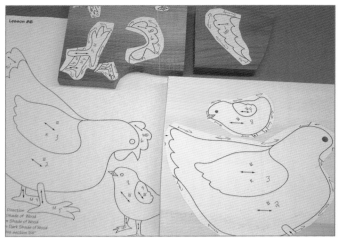

6.1

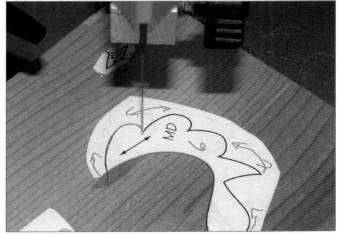

6.2

6.3

giving it about a ¼" border around the line work. Get another copy of the pattern and cut the rest of the parts (the MD tail and crest, the M feet and beak). Transfer the numbers from the master onto the copy.

Next get ready to glue the pattern to the wood. Get your wood as dust free as possible. I use a re-stickable glue stick. It is a water-based product that works great for me. A repositionable spray adhesive will do the job also. I trim any paper even with the edge of the board. Another thing that I like to do is mark arrows on all the outside edges. This way, when you start sawing, you can saw the outside edges first. Nothing fits next to the outside parts, so you can relax a bit and get into the swing of sawing before you have to make any parts fit **(see photo 6.1)**.

Scroll Sawing

Before beginning to saw the hen and the chick be sure to do the drilling for the eyes. This hen and chick have some interesting cuts to make. The feet are pretty basic on both and could be cut at anytime. The crest with beak on the mom chicken is a little tricky because of the sharp inside corners around the outside of the part. The tail section also has the same type of cuts. I choose to cut the inside part of the crest that joins the chicken first, but that section could be cut at any time. I enter the backside of the crest, but again either side could be cut first. I cut the first curve **(see photo 6.2)** until I come to the point and then back up and make a loop in the scrap piece **(see photo 6.3)**. After removing the loop piece, I back into the cut to where I stopped the first cut and then proceed to cut around the second hump. I repeat this until all the humps of the crest are sawed. Doing this should produce a sharp inside corner; however, if you miss the mark a little you can go back in and trim where necessary.

The same procedure can be used for the tail of the chicken. Caution must be used on the tail section

6.4

because another part has to fit against it. The wing in the body of the chicken and the chick are easy to cut because they are cut from the same wood and just go back together naturally. I normally do all of my cutting and save these kinds of cuts until the last. I use a smaller blade on these cuts to minimize the kerf width.

Checking for Fit

Before taking the paper off, it's a good idea to check the overall project to see if everything is fitting correctly. There may be some discrepancies where two sections meet. The line work on the pattern may reveal where the fit problem is. If there is not any line work evident and there is still a fit problem, you can make a mark on the part and trim it with the saw. We use a new sharp blade in the scroll saw to trim any parts if needed.

Shaping

Before removing the paper, transfer the number from the pattern to the back of the part. When you are satisfied with the fit, remove the paper **(see photo 6.4)**. At this stage, it is a good idea to take a minute and study the project again. I like to get a general idea of what I plan on doing. I start with the parts that make up the background, or the parts that would be the farthest from the viewer.

Here's The Plan

I use a sanding shim for the chicken, to sand areas consistently and make them at this time. Either use the pattern or trace around the parts to make the shim. The shim will support only a few parts: the medium dark tail and the white body of the chicken. If there are only a few parts, the sanding shim does not need to be the same size as the entire chicken. I will be using double-sided tape to stick the parts together on the sanding ¼" plywood shim. Now I will be able to sand the parts as if they were one piece of wood.

Also, I check to see if I can raise any areas by placing a shim under the wood to make some parts thicker. This can only be successfully done on interior parts. An exposed ¼" plywood shim on the side isn't very attractive. On the hen, I will raise the wing **(see photo 6.5)**. If I don't raise this part, I will need to sand the hen's body down to about ½" thick so the wing can be the thickest part. Many times raising parts will save some sanding time.

My plan is to start with the larger chicken first. The leg on the left, because it is in the background, will be the first part I sand. I'll take it down to about ¼" off the entire surface, because it joins the body and the right leg. Next comes the beak/crown on the hen's head; I'll sand it about ½" thick and then round the head down to that thickness. Then I'll sand the chicken's body with the sanding shim. Moving to the thickest parts, I'll sand the right foot. The last part is the wing.

On the little chicken, I'll follow a very similar process. I'll start with the left leg, because it's in the background. Then I'll do the right leg. The wing will be the thickest part of this piece, and because the wing is part of the outside edge, I cannot raise it very easily. This

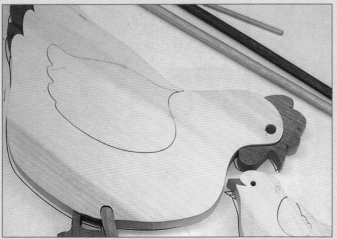

6.5

means I need to sand the entire body of the little chicken down to about ½" to make the wing be the thickest part at ¾". Next I'll mark the beak and sand it to match the body. The wing will remain thicker than the body; however, I will soften the edges so it doesn't appear to be just a flat step-up section. Remember to rough in the entire project and slowly bring it to completion.

Now to actually start the shaping follow the steps below.

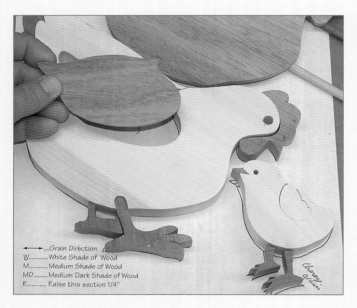

Step 1

Sand the legs on the little chick: the left one to about ¼" and the right one to about ⅜". Mark on the lower body where they join.

Step 2

Now let's move on to the main part of the chick. In order to make the wing stand out we will need to lower the chicken to at least ⅝" thick. Take this off the surface first then start rounding the outside edges. Round the belly area first. Make sure you don't round it below the pencil lines for the legs. Round the head down the back to soften all the outside edges.

Step 3

Put the beak in place and mark where the head meets the beak. Sand the beak down to this line to match the same thickness. You want the beak to look like it is coming out of the face.

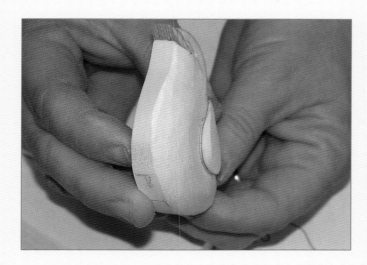

Step 4

Mark around the wing of the little chick and round the wing down toward the backside, leaving some thickness on the lower wing section.

Step 5

Move on to the hen. Sand the medium-dark beak/crest part next. Sand the entire beak/crest down to about a ½" thickness. Be sure to use your pencil and mark the parts just sanded.

Step 6

Sand the left leg down to about ⅜". With a pencil, mark where the leg section joins the body and the right leg/foot part.

Step 7

Prepare to sand the white body and the medium-dark tail pieces by turning the parts upside down. Start with the larger white part, then place the medium-dark section next to it. I place the parts upside-down so I can see exactly where I need to put my tape. Use at least two pieces of tape on each part to hold it down to the shim. Check to make sure your sanding shim is flat. Any warped pieces will make it almost impossible to keep your parts taped to the shim.

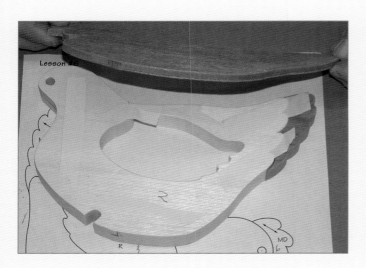

Step 8

When all the parts are secure, sand the body. Round the head down to the ½" thickness of the beak/crest pencil line. Round the body part on the belly area, being careful not to sand below the pencil line showing the thickness for the background left leg. Round the outside edge of the entire chicken except for the tail section. Leave the tail more flat. With the pieces still taped together, finish-sand where the medium-dark parts and the white parts join.

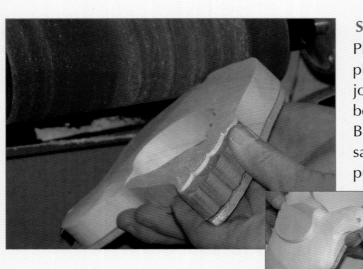

Step 9

Place the raising shim and wing section in place and mark with pencil where the body joins the wing. Follow a contour similar to the body, keeping the wing thicker than the body. Be sure to watch your pencil lines and don't sand below them. To add some more detail, put some grooves between the feathers. You can carve or sand these lines to give more definition between the feathers.

Step 10

Put the right foot in place and mark with your pencil where the body hits the leg. Sand the leg to match the pencil line you just made. This will make the leg look as though it is coming out of the body along the same plane.

Step 11

You can take the chicken off the sanding shim now. Both chickens are roughed in at this point. Go back and clean up all the parts and add more detail where needed.

Step 12

The larger chicken could use more detail sanding on the feet. Do some carving/sanding between the toes. Use an X-Acto knife or a small sander to get into these tight spaces. A very sharp blade in a utility knife will help to carve areas if you do not have any power tools to clean them out. The same detail can be added to the smaller chicken's feet.

Step 13

Soften the hard edges on the tail, crown and wings by sanding a small radius on the edges.

Step 14

Last but not least is the eye. Use a ⅛" and a ¼" dowel for the eyes. If you are using a light-colored dowel, round it first, then burn the exposed area. Slide the dowel in from the back and make a cut-off mark with a pencil. I like to glue the dowel in at this time to keep from losing it.

Step 15

Erase any pencil lines that may be showing and check again for any deep scratches.

Applying the Finish

Dust or blow off all the parts and apply the finish. Please refer to the finish section in Lesson One for basic instructions.

Make the Backing

After the gel has dried, you can make your backing from ¼" Luan plywood. (Please refer to the instructions in Lesson One.)

Glue the Chickens Down

On the hen, I use the hot glue on the crest/beak part to lock it in place. I use the hot glue combination on the leg in the foreground also. I use woodworkers glue on the rest of the parts. Using just dots of glue will be ample to hold the parts. I glue the wing last, gluing the shim first then gluing the wing on top of the shim. I use the woodworkers glue on the entire little chick. Allow the glue to set before putting on the hanger. For more details on gluing refer to the gluing section in Lesson One.

Put on the Hanger

For pictures and instructions on adding a hanger, see Lesson Eight.

Apple with Worm

Practice wood selection (using natural highlights in the wood), using a shim to raise a section, and a little carving to accentuate parts.

TOOLS:

- Scroll saw or bandsaw
- #5 reverse skip tooth blades
- Sander for contouring, (Softer is better. A pneumatic (air-inflated) sander is best, however a belt sander or disc sander will work also.)
- Carving knife or woodburner (optional)

MATERIALS:

- A light shade of wood at least 2" x 3" x ¾"
- A medium shade of wood at least 6" x 6" x ¾"
- A medium dark shade of wood at least 2" x 3" x ¾"
- A dark shade of wood at least 1" x 3" x ¾"
- Repositionable spray adhesive or glue stick
- At least five copies of the Apple and Worm pattern
- ¼" Luan plywood for the backing and raising shim
- ¹⁄₁₆" dowel for the eye
- ¹⁄₁₆" drill bit
- Woodworkers glue

Pattern Preparation/Layout

Glance over the pattern. The Apple with Worm has four colors of wood, and the grain direction goes all different ways. To make the apple you will need four copies: three for the pattern pieces and one for your master. Then it's good to have one extra copy just in case. Also, some clear tape is handy in case you make a cut in the wrong place. Five copies should be enough to complete the project.

I use at least ¾" thick wood and find wood grains/colors that will enhance the project.

We use Western red cedar, which comes somewhat smooth on the face and both edges. We run the rough side through a planer, taking off just enough wood so the piece lies flat. Clean up both sides if needed, but try to conserve the thickness of the wood. Many times I like to add a light source to a project. What I mean by this is to add highlighted wood to one side of the project. I'll put an arrow indicating where the light source is coming from **(see photo 7.2)**. Then, as I layout my parts, if I have wood that goes from a light shade to a darker shade, I'll put the lighter shade on the side with

PROJECT SPECS:

Finished size: 6³/₈" H by 5⁹/₁₆" W

Apple with Worm

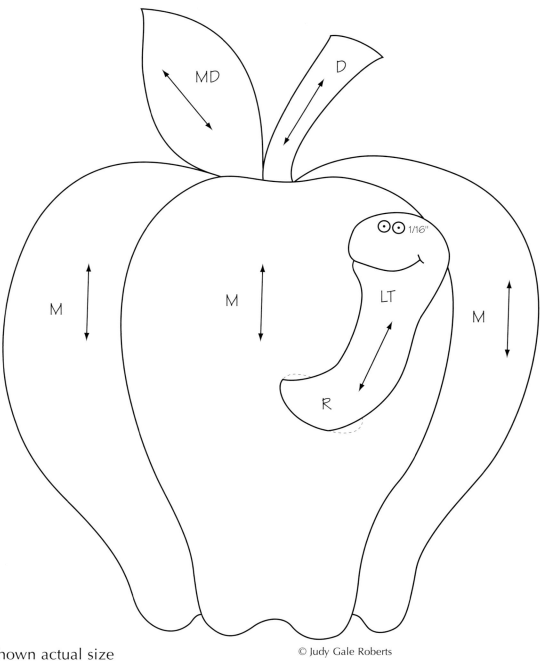

© Judy Gale Roberts

Pattern is shown actual size

⟵⟶ ....Grain Direction
LT............Light Shade of Wood
M........... Medium Shade of Wood
MD........Medium Dark Shade of Wood
D............ Dark Shade of Wood
R............Raise these areas 1/4"

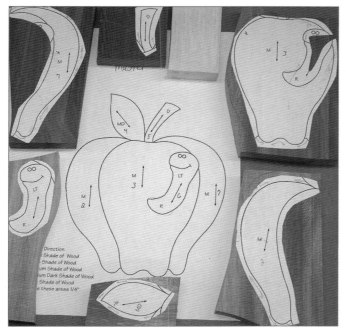

7.1

7.2

the arrow. This adds so much extra dimension to the finished project.

Label one of the pattern copies as your master. I like to number each part on the master. Next take one of the copies and cut out the M apple parts. If you plan to highlight one side of the apple, you may want to cut the sections individually. That is what I did. If you don't have the wood to do this, just cut the M apple parts and leave them as one section, trimming it to give it about a ¼" border around the line work. Then take another copy of the pattern and cut the worm and leaf out of it. You will need to cut the stem out of another copy of the pattern.

Next get ready to glue the pattern to the wood. Get your wood as dust free as possible. I use a re-stickable glue stick. It is a water-based product that works great for me. A repositionable spray adhesive will do the job also. I trim any paper even with the edge of the board. Another thing that I like to do is mark arrows on all the outside edges. This way, when you start sawing, you can saw the outside edges first. Nothing fits next to the outside parts, so you can relax a bit and get into the swing of sawing before you have to make any parts fit **(see photo 7.1)**.

Before you start sawing out your parts, the worm has ¹⁄₁₆" holes for the eyes that need to be drilled. It's a good idea to do any drilling before you start cutting the parts out.

Scroll Sawing

This apple is pretty basic to saw, but there is one area where caution should be taken. As you can see, the apple parts are all the same color and the same grain direction, so the project can be sawed out of the same wood. Be sure to do the drilling for the worm eyes before you begin sawing. Before I cut the apple, I drilled a hole in the worm area to thread my blade through. I then cut this area first, and after completing the cut, I set it aside and cut the worm out of LT wood. I then inserted the worm into its place in the apple just to make sure it fit before I cut the apple apart. If the worm does not fit, you can mark the apple and then trim the apple part with your scroll saw instead of the worm. There may be some cases where the worm has to be trimmed, but for the most part, I would rather trim the apple. After the worm fits in the apple, you can proceed with the rest of the apple. Saw all of the outside parts of the apple as well as the stem and leaf. Then use a smaller blade (#2 or smaller) to slice the apple into its parts.

The smile on the worm is a single blade width (normally I use a #5). At the end of the smile, you can make a quick turn and saw half of the cross section. I back out of the cut, then reverse the direction and back into the end of the section that I just cut. I cut the other short part last.

Checking for Fit

Before taking the paper off, it's a good idea to check the overall project to see if everything is fitting all correctly. On the apple, because we cut it out of the same piece of wood, there shouldn't be a fit problem. If you had to use two pieces of wood for the apple, there may be some discrepancies where the two sections meet. The line work on the pattern may reveal where the fit problem is. If there is not any line work evident and there is still a fit problem, you can make a mark on the part and trim it with the saw. We use a new sharp blade in the scroll saw to trim any parts if needed.

Shaping

Before removing the paper, make sure to transfer the number from the pattern to the back of the part. After the paper is removed, it is a good idea to take a minute and study the project again **(see photo 7.2)**. I like to get a general idea of what I plan on doing.

Here's The Plan

I start with the parts that make up the background, or the parts that would be the farthest from the viewer. This project doesn't need a sanding shim, but it does have a shim to raise the worm. Make your raising shim at this time. On the apple, my plan is to start with the leaf. I'll sand it down to about ¼". Next I'll do the stem, then the apple and last the worm. Remember to rough in the entire project and slowly bring it to a completion.

Now to actually start the shaping follow the steps below.

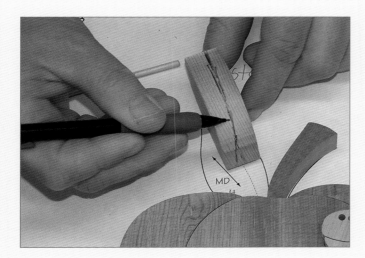

Step 1

Sand the leaf down to about ¼". Taper it down toward the top of the apple, maybe to about ⅛" thick. Sometimes it is easier to mark how much wood you want to take off, then you will have a guide when you start sanding.

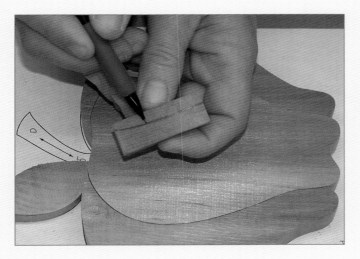

Step 2

Next mark where the leaf joins the stem and the apple. Taper the stem down toward the apple. Stay just above the pencil line drawn from the leaf.

Step 3

Mark with a pencil where the stem joins the apple.

Step 4

If you have any apples around the house, it would be a great to have one next to you as you sand the wood apple. You'll note the top part of the apple has a larger diameter than the bottom part. To create this look, take some wood off the lower part of the apple. I found it's better to take the surface wood off first, then round the edges. When parts are rounded it is harder to see the thickness. I always recommend sanding the various thicknesses before you start contouring any of the parts. This will ensure that you have a variety of depths and will make your project much more dimensional in the long run.

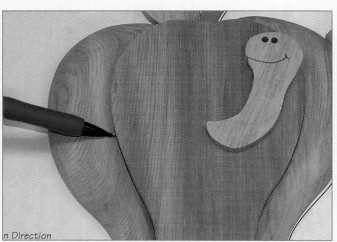

Step 5

First lower the left and the right sides of the apple down to about ½" thick, then taper them down toward the bottom. Start rounding the outside edges. Watch your pencil lines for the stem and leaf parts. Stay above these lines. Since this is a free-form project, you can round the apple all the way down the outside edges. If the project had a part that joined the outside edge, you wouldn't want to sand the outside edges. Put these two outer sections back in place and mark with your pencil where they join.

Step 6

Taper the middle apple section down toward the bottom, then round down to the pencil lines on the sides. Stay above the pencil lines, otherwise you will need to lower the outer apple sections. This section is ¾" thick at the center and rounded toward the edges.

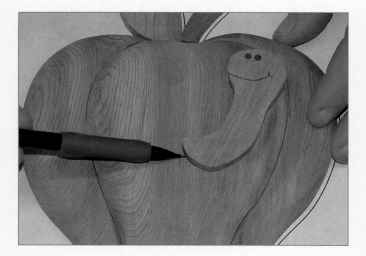

Step 7

After the apple is roughed in, the worm is ready to be roughed in. Put the ¼" shim in place and slide the worm in place. With your pencil, mark where the apple joins the worm. The worm's head will be the thickest part of the worm. Taper the worm down to the pencil line where the end of the worm meets the apple. You want the worm to appear to be coming out of the apple. Round the worm down to the pencil lines, leaving the head a knob-like shape. At this point the project is roughed in. The head of the worm is close to 1" thick— where it joins the apple it's about ¾" thick.

Step 8

Mark the stem if the thickness of the leaf has changed. Roll the stem right to the leaf line. The top and outside edge can be sanded clean and rounded down to the outside edge.

Step 9

Mark the apple if the stem and leaf thicknesses changed. Sand the apple with the grain to give it a very smooth appearance.

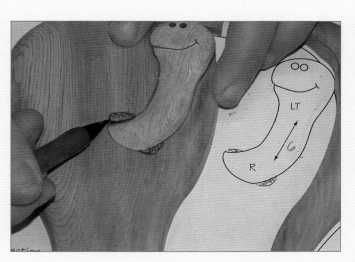

Step 10

You can carve, burn or sand the area around the worm's hole. This area is indicated by dashed lines on the pattern. A combination of carving and burning would look great. Using a sharp knife or a rotary hand tool, carve small dips where the dashed lines are. This alone will look great.

Step 11

Put the worm back in place and mark the sides of the worm if more wood is exposed after carving the dips for the hole. This pencil line will show you if you need to clean up more of the exposed sides of the worm.

Step 12

Moving up to the face, I like to add some definition to the smile. Carve the lower portion of the smile, a ¹⁄₃₂" or so, just enough to make the smile stand out. Use a sharp knife, rotary power tool, or hand sanding.

Step 13

Last but not least are the eyes. Use a ⅛" dowel for the eyes. If you are using a light-colored dowel, round it first, then burn the exposed area. Slide the dowel in from the backside and mark the cut-off point with a pencil. I like to glue the dowel after cutting it to length.

Step 14

Erase any pencil lines that may be showing and check again for any deep scratches. Sand all the outside edges. Because this is a freeform project, you can roll the apple all the way to the lower edge.

Applying the Finish

Dust or blow off all the parts and apply the finish. Please refer to the finishing section for Lesson One.

Make the Backing

After the gel has dried, you can make your backing from ¼" Luan plywood. (Please refer to the instructions in Lesson One.)

Glue the Apple and Worm Down

I use the hot glue/woodworkers glue combination on both outside parts of the apple. Be careful if using both types of glue, because the woodworkers glue can cool the hot glue too fast if they touch. Then I use the woodworkers glue on the rest of the parts. Using just dots of glue will be ample to hold the parts. When I glue projects that have raising shims, I glue all the parts around the raised parts first. This will ensure that the shim will go in the right place. Glue the shim in, then glue the worm in place. Allow the glue to set before putting on the hanger. For more details on gluing refer to the gluing section in Lesson One.

Put on the Hanger

For pictures and instructions on adding a hanger, see Lesson Eight.

Hot Air Balloon

In this lesson you will get to practice making a project very dimensional and choosing a piece of wood that goes from a light to dark for the balloon. Use a mirror hanger to hang your projects on the wall.

TOOLS:

- Scroll saw or bandsaw
- #5 reverse skip tooth blades
- Sander for contouring, (Softer is better. A pneumatic (air-inflated) sander is best, however a belt sander or disc sander will work also.)
- Carving knife or woodburner (optional)

MATERIALS:

- A light shade of wood at least 1" x 2" x ¾"
- A medium shade of wood at least 7½" x 9" x ¾"
- A medium dark shade of wood at least 1" x 2" x ¾"
- Repositionable spray adhesive or glue stick
- At least four copies of the Hot Air Balloon pattern
- ¼" Luan plywood for the backing and raising shim
- Woodworkers glue

Pattern Preparation/Layout

Glance over the pattern. The Hot Air Balloon has three colors of wood. To make this project you will need four copies of the pattern: three for the pattern pieces and one for your master. Then it's good to have one extra copy just in case. Five copies should be enough to complete the project.

I use at least ¾" thick wood and find wood grains/colors that will enhance the project.

We use Western red cedar, which comes somewhat smooth on the face and both edges. We run the rough side through a planer, taking off just enough wood so the piece lies flat. Clean up both sides if needed, but try to conserve the thickness of the wood. I use aspen for any areas I want to be white or for the lightest part of the project. Use whatever wood you have on hand for this project.

Label one of the pattern copies as your master. I like to number each part on the master. Next take one of the copies and cut the entire balloon section (if the color and grain direction are the same they can be laid out in one section). Trim it, giving it about a ¼" border

PROJECT SPECS:

Finished size: 9¹³/₁₆" H by 7" W

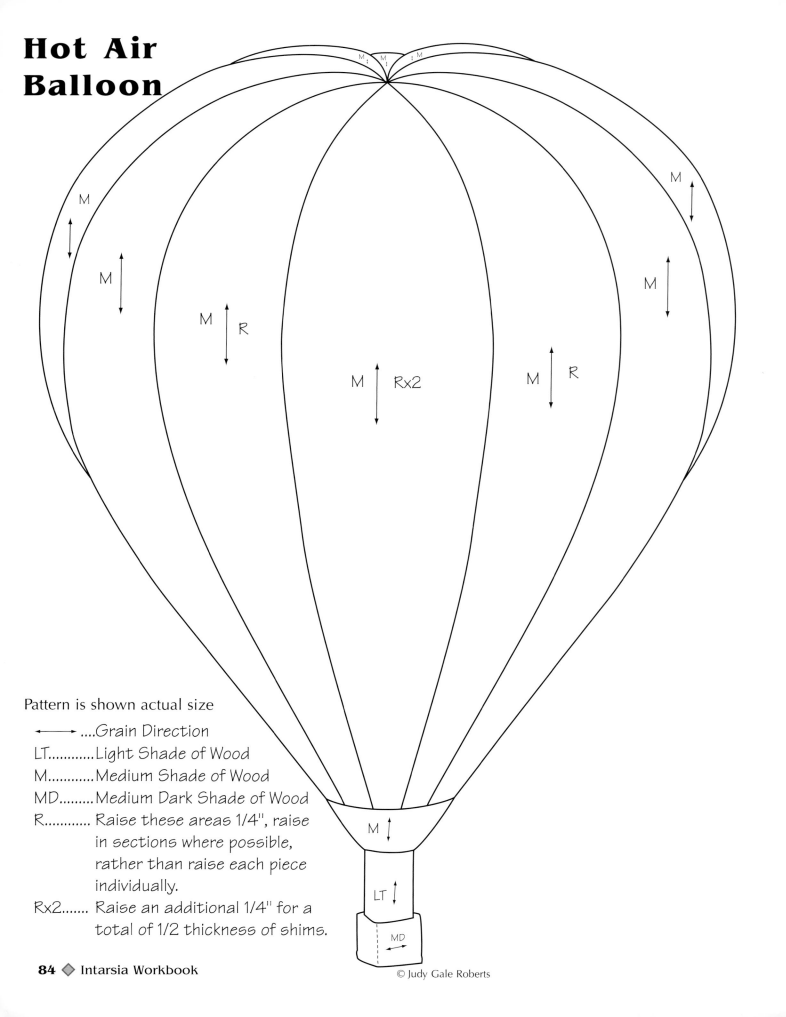

Hot Air Balloon

Pattern is shown actual size

←——→ ....Grain Direction

LT............Light Shade of Wood

M............Medium Shade of Wood

MD........Medium Dark Shade of Wood

R............ Raise these areas 1/4", raise in sections where possible, rather than raise each piece individually.

Rx2....... Raise an additional 1/4" for a total of 1/2 thickness of shims.

around the line work. Get another copy out and cut the LT section, and then one more copy to cut the MD basket part. Transfer the numbers from the master to the pattern pieces.

Next get ready to glue the pattern onto the wood. Get your wood as dust free as possible. I use a re-stickable glue stick. It is a water-based product that works great for me. A repositionable spray adhesive will do the job also. I trim any paper even with the edge of the board. Another thing that I like to do is mark arrows on all the outside edges. This way, when you start sawing, you can saw the outside edges first. Nothing fits next to the outside parts, so you can relax a bit and get into the swing of sawing before you have to make any parts fit.

Scroll Sawing

The Balloon is a very simple project to saw. Just cut out the outside part of the balloon and then the bottom parts. After all parts have been cut, then you can change to a smaller blade and slice up the balloon parts. The only tricky areas are the small balloon parts at the very top.

If you would like the balloon to be striped, just alter the colors. Care must then be taken when sawing out the differently colored stripes to assure that the parts fit.

Checking for Fit

Before taking the paper off, it's a good idea to check the overall project to see if everything is fitting correctly. If you cut the balloon out of the same piece of wood there shouldn't be a fit problem. If you had to use two pieces of wood, there may be some discrepancies where the two sections meet. The line work on the pattern may reveal where the fit problem is. If there is not any line work evident and there is still a fit problem, you can make a mark on the part and trim it with the saw. We use a new sharp blade in the scroll saw to trim any parts if needed.

Shaping

Before removing the paper make sure to transfer the number from the pattern to the back of the part. At this stage, it is a good idea to take a minute and study the project again. I like to get a general idea of what I plan on doing. I start with the parts that make up the background, or the parts that would be the farthest from the viewer.

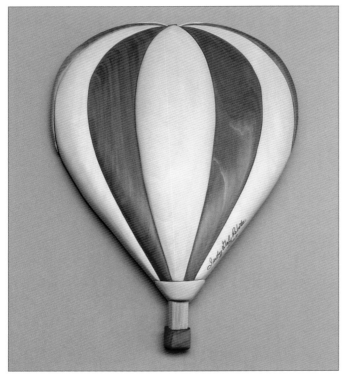

Alter the colors to create a striped balloon.

Here's The Plan

I use two shims on this project to give the balloon a more rounded shape, and I make them at this time. The sections marked R are raised ¼", and the part marked Rx2 is raised an additional ¼", making it a total of ½". First make one shim that will raise all three middle sections. Then make one shim to raise the one part in the middle. On the balloon, my plan is to start with the lowest part of the balloon first. Then I'll come back and sand the ribs between the sections. When the balloon is roughed in, I'll start on the lower basket section.

Now to actually start the shaping follow the steps below.

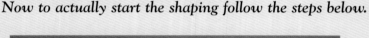

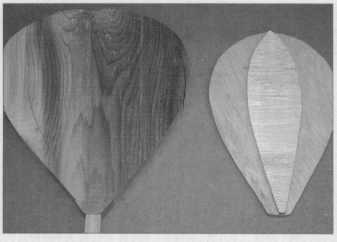

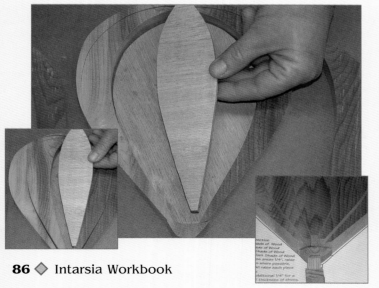

Step 1

Put the raising shims in place to help visualize the depth. First I will round the lower rim-like part on the bottom of the balloon. This area requires a little extra caution. Do not sand the center part of this piece lower than ½". The very center of the rim-like piece covers the two raising shims. It is a good idea to mark on the inside of the rim-like part to limit how much wood to remove. Round the rim-like part, put it back in place and mark the lower sections of the balloon. By rounding this part first it will give you a guide for the lower ribs of the balloon.

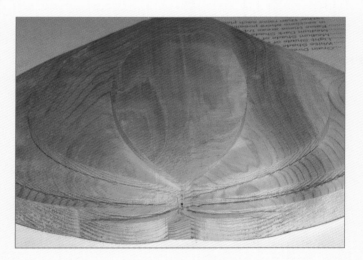

Step 2

At this point, I will start on the top part. It is the farthest from the viewer. Lower the smallest part on the top to about ⅜". Do not round any parts yet, as mentioned before it is much easier to visualize the depth if you leave it flat. Mark where that part joins the two adjoining parts. Sand these parts to around ⅝" thick. The next section will stay ¾", the following sections will be 1" (with ¼" shim), and the last section (with the extra shim) will be 1¼" thick with the two ¼" shims.

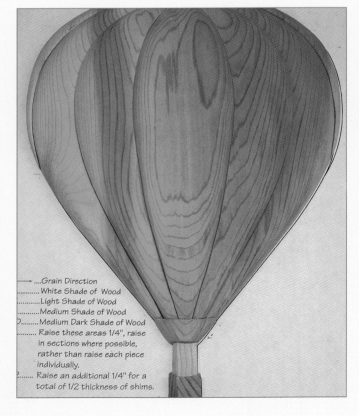

Step 3

Now start tapering the ribs down to the rim-like part that was sanded earlier. Taper the parts down to the pencil line. After the levels are achieved, start rounding the outside edges. Be careful not to round the edges down too far. Stop at the pencil line. The softer the curve you sand, the more pillow-soft the balloon will look. We are striving for a billowing, air-filled balloon look.

Step 4

Now sand the little basket. I put a sharp angle off center using the dashed line on the pattern as a guide for the angles. The light section in between these two parts is sanded to about ¼" thick.

Step 5

After all have been shaped, go back and sand all the parts with the grain, using a rougher 180-grit at first. Then go over all the parts with 220-grit sandpaper. Erase any pencil lines and prepare to put the finish on.

→ ....Grain Direction
.... White Shade of Wood
.... Light Shade of Wood
.... Medium Shade of Wood
D......... Medium Dark Shade of Wood
.... Raise these areas 1/4", raise
      in sections where possible,
      rather than raise each piece
      individually.
.......Raise an additional 1/4" for a
      total of 1/2 thickness of shims.

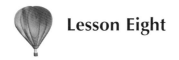

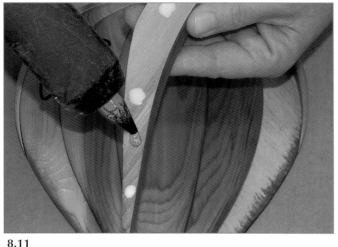

8.11

8.12

8.13

8.14

Applying the Finish

Dust or blow off all the parts and apply the finish. Please refer to the finishing section in Lesson One.

Make the Backing

After the gel has dried, you can make your backing from ¼" Luan plywood. (Please refer to the instructions in Lesson One.)

Glue the Balloon Down

I glue the rim-like part at the base of the balloon first. It is rather small, so I just put two dots of woodworkers glue and one dot of hot glue in the center. Locking this part down gives a base to glue the rest of the balloon parts without losing placement. I used woodworkers glue and hot glue on the longer ribs of the balloon. Put the woodworkers glue on first leaving space for the hot glue (see photo 8.11). Be careful if you are using

both types of glue, because the woodworkers glue can cool the hot glue too fast if it touches. When I glue projects that have raising shims, I glue all the parts around the raised parts first. This will ensure that the shim will go in the right place. Glue the first shim in (see photo 8.12), then glue the ribs of the balloon, and then the final shim (see photo 8.13). I use just woodworkers glue on all of the smaller parts. Using just dots of glue will be ample to hold the small parts. I glue the small parts and allow them time to dry. Allow the glue to set before putting on the hanger.

Put on the Hanger

There are many different ways to hang the projects. We use a method that has proven to be strong and reliable and is also adjustable. You could use a Saw Tooth hanger, but more times than not, the project seems to hang crooked. We have found the best thing is to use a Mirror Hanger, which can be found at many home cen-

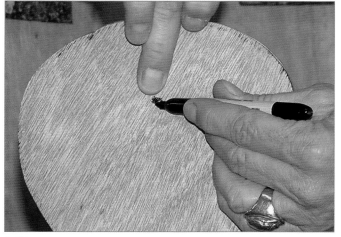

8.15

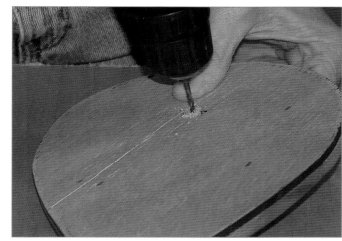

8.16

8.17

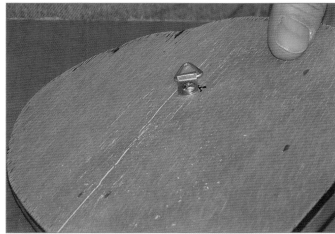

8.18

ters and hardware stores. Mirror hangers come in many different sizes. For the projects in this book we used a small mirror hanger.

Regardless of the method used, we have to find out where the center of the project is. To do this, I pinch the project between my thumb and middle finger **(see photo 8.14)** and let it hang between my fingers. I change the location of my fingers until the desired location is found. Once I find the desired location, I will mark the backing right at my fingertip **(see photo 8.15)**. This is where I will drill a hole for the screw. I always drill the hole just slightly smaller than the screw I use, which is a #6 X ½" sheet metal screw **(see photo 8.16)**. I mark my drill for the depth to make sure I don't drill all the way through the project. Just make sure that the area you choose to drill is at least ⅝" thick. Bear in mind that the backing we used is ¼" thick, so you will only be drilling into the actual piece about ¼".

After drilling the hole you can install the mirror

hanger **(see photo 8.17)**. I don't tighten the screw too much, but it still needs to be snug, because I want the hanger to be able to swivel from right to left **(see photo 8.18)**. This allows me to adjust the project so it will hang straight on the wall.

INTARSIA PATTERNS available from Judy Gale Roberts • Roberts Studio

2620 HEATHER RD • SEYMOUR, TN 37865 • 1 (800) 316-9010 • (865) 428-8875 • FAX (865) 428-7870
FOR A MORE DETAILED DESCRIPTION WITH PICTURES OF THE FOLLOWING PATTERNS,
PLEASE WRITE OR CALL THE ABOVE ADDRESS AND ASK FOR A COPY OF THE "INTARSIA TIMES."

PANDA	MANATEE	GIRAFFE	CAT ON SHELF
TOUCAN	POLAR BEAR	COYOTE	FOOTBALL PLAYER
RACCOON	TIGER	STILL POTTERY	WOOD DUCK
CAT IN BAG	ELEPHANT	WOLF	GERMAN SHEPARD
SEASCAPE	BLACK RHINO	OL' BLUE	BLACK GEAR
ROSE	SANTA	FAWN AND DOE	MARE & FOWL
CAT WITH YARN	WREATH	WHITE TAIL DEER	GREVY'S ZEBRA
KOALA BEARS	DOLPHIN	CHRISTMAS SIGN	PRAYING HANDS
BIG FOOT CLOWN	PENGUINS	ANGEL	KITTEN AND BEAR
CLOWN IN WINDOW	DOG	ASIAN LION	PRONGHORN
CLOWN WITH DAISIES	U S A EAGLE	BARN	CROSS WITH DOVE
BUCK DEER	COW	GOLFER	LONGHORN
HORSE	BEARS	BATTER UP	SQUIRREL
BUTTERFLY AND ORCA	SWAN	CASTLE	UNICORN
OH HOOT WEST	SAIL BOAT	ROOSTER WEATHER VEIN	CANADIAN GANDER
MOUSE	ARIZONA	BALD EAGLE	CANADIAN GOOSE
CHRISTMAS STOCKINGS	UP CARROUSEL	ELK	HOWLING WOLF
PELICAN	DOWN CARROUSEL	HUMMING BIRD	INDIAN FACE
HOBO CLOWN	CAMEL	COVERED BRIDGE	CHRISTMAS CANDLES
FLAMINGOS	ROSE BUD	CHRISTMAS STOCKING #2	BIG HORN
STILL LIFE	BARN OWL	CARDINALS	COTTON TAIL
LIGHT HOUSE	WABBIT	WOMAN GOLFER	ST. FRANCIS
BALLOON	TROPICAL FISH	FRUIT STILL LIFE	CARIBOU
DUCK	ANTIQUE SANTA	COWBOY	HUNTIN' BUDDIES
PIG IN A BLANKET	CHRISTMAS ORNAMENTS	PUP WITH DECOY	FEATHERED FRIENDS
BAG LADY	OH HOOT HAWAIIAN	RING NECK PHEASANT	MOM'S KITCHEN
CURIOUS COON	ROCKY TOP	RED FOX	WHITE PELICAN
BASS	CALLAS FLOWER	SNOWMAN & CHICKADEE	GRANDPA'S ANGEL
CAT IN CHAIR	FLORIDA PANTHER	NOAH'S ARK	NATURE BOY
BOG BUDDIES	MOOSE	SUN FLOWER WELCOME	CARDINAL & DOGWOOD

**THE PATTERNS ABOVE ARE PRINTED FULL SIZE ON 17 1/2" x 23" TRANSPARENT TRACING PAPER,
EACH PATTERN COMES WITH A 8" x 10" COLOR PRINT OF THE FINISHED PROJECT.
THE PATTERNS ABOVE SELL FOR $7.95 EACH OR 3 FOR $21.95 PLUS $6.00 SHIPPING.**

EAGLE	WOODLAND TRAIL	SEA GULL PILING	INDIAN WOMAN
CLOUD NINE	EAGLE LANDING	BUFFALO	MACAW PARADISE
LAST SUPPER	INDIAN	ON A LIMB COON	ALLIGATOR DREAMS
	OWL		

**THE PATTERNS ABOVE ARE PRINTED FULL SIZE ON 25" x 38" TRANSPARENT TRACING PAPER,
EACH PATTERN COMES WITH A 8" x 10" BLACK AND WHITE PRINT OF THE FINISHED PROJECT.
THE LARGER SIZE PATTERNS ABOVE SELL FOR $8.95 EACH OR 3 FOR $24.95**

Buy one or all of the patterns available for just one shipping charge of $6.00.

- THREE POSTER PATTERN SETS, "THE HIDDEN FOREST", "NEW SHOES", AND "AFRICAN ADVENTURE" EACH SET COMES WITH A PATTERN AND A 19" x 25" FULL COLOR POSTER SUITABLE FOR FRAMING. $24.95 EACH PLUS $6.00 SHIPPING. $6.50 FOR CANADIAN RESIDENTS.
- "FAMILY AFFAIR" COMES WITH 13" x 19" COLOR POSTER AND THE FINISHED FRAME SIZE IS 32.5" x 38". $19.95 EACH PLUS $6.00 SHIPPING.
- A 90 MINUTE INTARSIA INSTRUCTIONAL VIDEO WHICH COVERS A BEGINNER LEVEL PATTERN FROM START TO FINISH.

If you are interested in receiving our free newsletter called the "Intarsia Times," which lists over 225 patterns, please call or write to: Roberts Studio, 2620 Heather Rd., Seymour, TN 37865, (865) 428-8875, (800) 316-9010, jerry@intarsia.com, www.intarsia.com

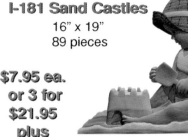

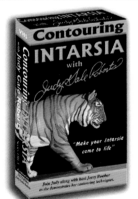
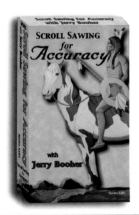

More Great Project Books from Fox Chapel Publishing

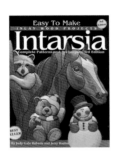

Easy To Make Inlay Wood Projects Intarsia - 3rd Edition
Complete Patterns & Techniques
by Judy Gale Roberts, Jerry Booher
Pages: 216
ISBN: 1-56523-126-0
$19.95

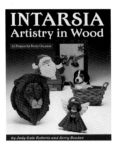

Intarsia: Artistry In Wood
12 Projects for Every Occasion
by Judy Gale Roberts, Jerry Booher
Pages: 72
ISBN: 1-56523-096-5
$14.95

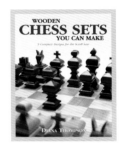

Wooden Chess Sets You Can Make
9 Complete Designs for the Scroll Saw
by Diana Thompson
Pages: 72
ISBN: 1-56523-188-0
$14.95

Scroll Saw Workbook 2nd Edition
Learn to Use Your Scroll Saw in 25 Skill-Building Chapters
by John A. Nelson
Pages: 92
ISBN: 1-56523-207-0
$14.95

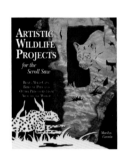

Artistic Wildlife Projects for the Scroll Saw
Bears, Wild Cats, Birds of Prey and Other Predators from Around the World
by Marilyn Carmin
Pages: 120
ISBN: 1-56523-224-0
$19.95

Words of Faith in Wood
53 Artistic Patterns for the Scroll Saw
by Jeff Paxton
Pages: 72
ISBN: 1-56523-228-3
$14.95

LOOK FOR THESE BOOKS AT YOUR LOCAL BOOK STORE OR WOODWORKING RETAILER
Or call 800-457-9112 • Visit www.FoxChapelPublishing.com

Learn from the Experts

Fox Chapel Publishing is not only your leading resource for woodworking books, we also publish the two leading how-to magazines for woodcarvers and woodcrafters!

WOOD CARVING ILLUSTRATED is the leading how-to magazine for woodcarvers of all skill levels and styles—providing inspiration and instruction from some of the world's leading carvers and teachers. A wide range of step-by-step projects are presented in an easy-to-follow format, with great photography and useful tips and techniques. *Wood Carving Illustrated* delivers quality editorial on the most popular carving styles, such as realistic and stylized wildlife carving, power carving, Santas, caricatures, chip carving and fine art carving. The magazine also includes tool reviews, painting and finishing features, profiles on carvers, photo galleries and more.

SCROLL SAW WORKSHOP is the leading how-to magazine for novice and professional woodcrafters. Shop-tested projects are complete with patterns and detailed instructions. The casual scroller appreciates the in-depth information that ensures success and yields results that are both useful and attractive; the pro will be creatively inspired with fresh and innovative design ideas. Each issue of *Scroll Saw Workshop* contains useful news, hints and tips, and includes lively features and departments that bring the world of scrolling to the reader.

Want to learn more about a subscription? **Visit www.FoxChapelPublishing.com** and click on either the *Wood Carving Illustrated* button or *Scroll Saw Workshop* button at the top of the page. Watch for our special **FREE ISSUE** offer! Or call toll-free at 1-800-457-9112.